origami quilts

origami quilts

20 folded fabric projects

Louise Mabbs and
Wendy Lowes

Dedicated to Ruth Hodgson (neé Withers) an inspirational, creative, woman who survived breast cancer, but died far too young in an untimely car accident while I was writing this book. LM

Dedicated to my husband, David, who has been extremely patient and supportive during the time that I have been writing and creating the projects. WL

First published in United States in 2006 by
Martingale & Company
20205 144th Ave. NE
Woodinville, WA 98072-8478 USA
www.martingale-pub.com

Commissioning editor: Marie Clayton
Designer: Louise Leffler
Photography: Michael Wicks
Printed in Singapore
11 10 09 08 07 06   6 5 4 3 2 1

Library of Congress Cataloging-in-Publication Data is available.
ISBN: 1-56477-624-7

Mission Statement
Dedicated to providing quality products and service to inspire creativity.

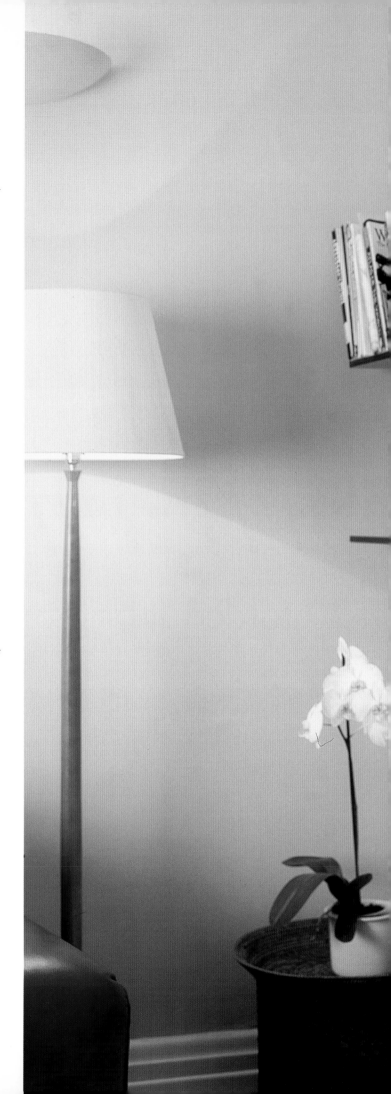

contents

introduction

I have sewn since I was a very young child—one of my mother's earliest recollections of my childhood was of me being in the "pin tin" at age two. My Godfather gave me my first origami book when I was ten and my Aunt, who was a needlework teacher, also encouraged me in all sorts of arts and crafts, so I have always "manipulated" things. At thirteen I decided to make a career in textiles and although I'm not a fashion designer as intended, I'm always looking for new ideas and new ways to stretch my skills.

I trained in constructed textiles at Winchester School of Art in England, where, after discovering and becoming addicted to quilts in 1983, I joined the Quilters' Guild, and later the Embroiderers' Guild. The origami influence was resurrected in 1988 when Gill Tanner organized an exhibition in Greens Mill Science Centre, Sneinton—a remodelled windmill in Nottinghamshire, England—on the theme of 'Wind'. My Origami Winds piece, done for this exhibition, was an interpretation of children's windmill toys.

In 1986 I became self-employed, making curtains, cushions and anything else in fabric that people wanted for their homes. When I got married, I concentrated on quilt commissions and studying for an adult teaching certificate. While my children were in preschool I started to dream of all the books I wanted to write, so when Marie approached me at the first Festival of Quilts I was thrilled. Top of my

mind was a book of quilts based on Fibonacci principles— mathematically-minded readers will spot that one Fibonacci project has crept into this book (one of the Twist and Grout cushions). However, Marie was interested in my samples of fabric folding ideas and wanted a book based around these, so then I asked Wendy to work with me.

I first met Wendy when she gave a talk to the London Embroiderers' Guild, and in 1999 I invited her to talk to the group I run in London, Around The Commons Textile Group, because I was intrigued by her paper origami demonstration. For years I had intended to join the British Origami Society—I finally achieved it a few months before we signed the contract for this book. At that point I had still only made one true origami quilt!

This book has been tremendous hard work for me. Wendy has been practising folded fabric techniques for years, while mine have developed and blossomed over a very steep six-month learning curve. I've thoroughly enjoyed creating these new techniques though, and hope you enjoy discovering them too.

So now to my Fibonacci book... Happy twisting!

Louise Mabbs, London 2005

introduction

Many years ago, when I was taught how to do Cathedral Window Patchwork, the act of folding squares reminded me of the origami that I used to do when I was a child and it occurred to me that it might be possible to use some of the same paper-folding techniques with fabric. To start myself off, I acquired some straightforward, well-illustrated "how to" books on origami, which taught me how to "read" origami diagrams and the names of all the different ways of folding—mountains and valleys, squash folds and petal folds for example.

Because I was aiming to make three-dimensional patchwork—rather than models of birds and animals—I was attracted to geometric designs. All origami models are illustrated with a series of step-by-step diagrams showing the sequence of folding and, by looking at these more carefully, I found that sometimes there were very interesting geometric shapes created in the middle of the sequence. I could just fold up to this point, and then join the pieces together, and no-one would ever know that I was half way to a dinosaur or a Chinese junk! I practised for ages with pieces of paper before trying it out with fabric—my experiments with design are all in shoe boxes rather than sketchbooks!

At first I only looked at books written in English but, after a while, I realized that the symbols used in the diagrams, like the notation of music, were the same all over the world, so I have now accumulated a number of origami books in different languages. As a member of Origami Societies in both Britain and America, I have attended a number of International Origami conventions where I have met and made friends with folders from many different parts of the world.

Having mastered the art of folding paper, I turned my attention to my real love, which is working with textiles. Obviously, cloth has quite different properties to paper, such as fraying edges and the bias effect when folding on the diagonal, and over the last fourteen years I have discovered what can and what cannot be folded in fabric. Sometimes the difference between fabric and paper is an advantage and I have been able to develop simpler ways of folding than those shown in origami books. Many of my folding sequences have developed from the same basic first folds and several will be shown in this book.

Origami is a Japanese word made up from *ori*, "to fold", and *gami*, "paper." One day, I went into a Japanese bookshop and asked the assistant what the Japanese word was for cloth or fabric. She told me it was *nuno*; so I said, "I do Orinuno." She replied, "There is no such thing!" but I said, "There is now!"

Wendy Lowes, London 2005

folded patchwork from around the world

Since the invention of the loom in about 4000 BC, in Egypt, people have been using woven fabric in many different ways. It was not long before people realized that folding the fabric added to its strength, warmth and decorative qualities. Archaeologists have found folded and pleated fabrics in ancient Egyptian tombs. Throughout history and today, in many parts of the world, pieces of folded cloth are put together to make a wide variety of patchwork objects. Modern forms of transport have made it easy to travel far and wide, so more people are seeing and collecting textiles from other cultures.

One of the most widely-spread folding techniques is that of Mitered or Quill patchwork, where small squares or rectangles of fabric are folded into triangles and then sewn down to a backing fabric in an overlapping pattern. Some of these are very tiny, such as those done by the Lisu Hill Tribes of Thailand.

The same effect can be achieved more easily by folding a length of ribbon, tape or fabric into a series of small triangles. This is commonly known as Saw-toothed Edging, Prairie Points or, in the Netherlands, *Muizentandjes* (Mouse Teeth). In India, triangular folded patchwork is often seen on the decorative straps made for animals on ceremonial occasions. The same technique in Russia, at the turn of the 19th/20th century, was mostly used for potholders. Sometimes, for extra strength, the folded triangles are folded in half again. In Belo Horizonte, Brazil, a large version using the double-folded method is used to make bath mats. The long, folded triangles are stitched down along their shortest sides onto the background fabric, leaving the long points free. The finished effect looks rather like feathers.

Above top: Small sample of the work of the Lisu Hill Tribes, of Thailand. Collection of Wendy Lowes.

Above: Section of folded patchwork decoration from a horsestrap. Kathiawar, India. Collection of Wendy Lowes.

Left: A Chinese oven glove, with Quill patchwork 'fur'. Collection of Louise Mabbs.

In the 19th century, probably due to missionary travels around the world, knowledge of these techniques arrived in Great Britain and America. In England, it is sometimes called Somerset patchwork and in the USA, Folded Star patchwork—see page 17.

Another ancient folded-fabric technique that has traveled across the world is the one that we know in the West as Cathedral Window. This technique has been known in China for hundreds of years. We can't determine exactly how long, because it has been passed down from mothers to daughters for generations, without diagrams or written instructions. In China, it is called the Lucky Coin or Ancient Coin design and can be found, most often, on purses and baby-carriers, as a symbol of wealth and good fortune. The name comes from the pattern of overlapping circle shapes that appear in the finished patchwork, resembling ancient Chinese coins, which were round with a square hole in the middle.

Above left: Somerset patchwork cushion, by Jean Martin.

Left: Bai baby carrier. The square panel in the lower section is Cathedral Window patchwork, with the addition of small decorative beads. Collection of Louise Mabbs.

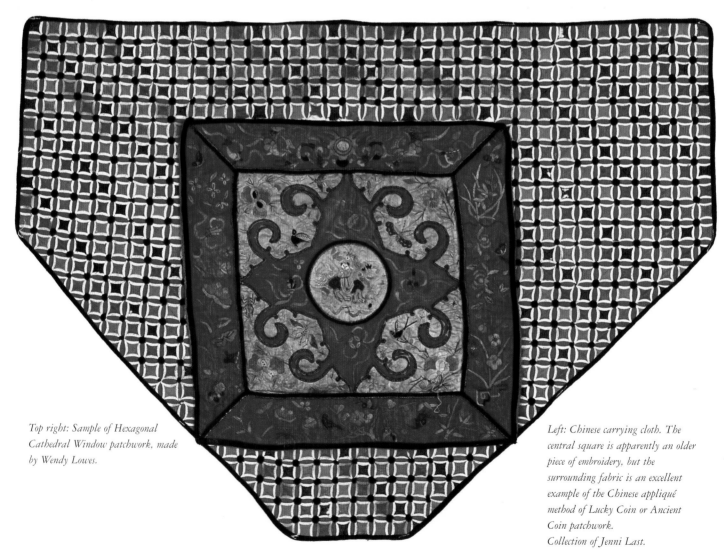

Top right: Sample of Hexagonal Cathedral Window patchwork, made by Wendy Lowes.

Left: Chinese carrying cloth. The central square is apparently an older piece of embroidery, but the surrounding fabric is an excellent example of the Chinese appliqué method of Lucky Coin or Ancient Coin patchwork.
Collection of Jenni Last.

Some beautiful silk wrapping cloths (*Chogakpo Pojagi, Cintamani*) were made in the nineteenth century in Korea, using the same technique.

The Chinese have also developed a quicker, less fabric-hungry way of getting the same effect, by folding small squares and applying them to a background fabric, as on the carrying cloth shown below opposite. The method of doing this is shown on page 16. Another method of producing the overlapping circle pattern is by making bagged circles of fabric and folding the edges down over a square shape, which is known as Japanese Folded Patchwork—see pages 16 and 17.

In 1992, Wendy Lowes experimented with folding hexagons, using the Cathedral Window technique—although, in fact, it can be done with any tessellating shapes. In the 1980's and 1990's, some quilters in the UK began to experiment with the Cathedral Window folded base squares, without the colored patches. They joined the folded squares together and then folded the top triangular flaps in various different ways achieving a bas-relief sculptural effect, as seen in Sheena Norquay's quilt below, which was made in 1991. Jennie Rayment is another

English textile artist who achieves a similar sculptural effect with amazing combinations of tucks and pleats. In the 1970's and 1980's, Wendy Whitfield, Louise Mabbs and Irene Ord independently experimented with cutting and folding back squares within several layers of fabric. Also in the 1980's, Julie Richardson and Linda Kemshall developed the pinch and pin method of twist-folding fabric, which is shown on page 64. The well-known Caryl Bryer Fallert made a series of over 300 stunning High Tech Tuck quilts in the 1980's and 1990's, using the folded flat piping method shown on page 20.

In 1993, Wendy Lowes began her fabric folding experiments using origami techniques, firstly in plain, unbleached calico and then in double-color squares with decorative stitched edges. The examples below show how different two panels can look, even though they are the same size and folded the same way.

Since then, also independently, at least two quilters in California, Rebecca Wat and Mary Jo Hiney, have used origami techniques in their work, but in quite different ways from the projects in this book. It is very exciting how new folding ideas keep developing all the time.

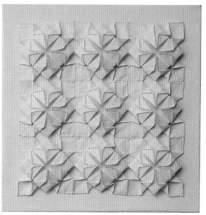

Above: Section of a quilt made in 1991 by Sheena Norquay. Courtesy Sheena Norquay.

Above right and right: Two panels by Wendy Lowes folded in exactly the same way, but looking very different due to the materials used.

traditional folding techniques

◂ log cabin: folded method, sunshine & shadow layout

By placing dark colors on two adjacent sides and light colors on the other adjacent sides, you can create fabulous optical illusions across a quilt.

VARIATIONS:

Off-Center – uses different widths of logs, but you need to work out on paper first where to put the 'center' square.

Random Log Cabin – uses this technique, but adding any width of log until the backing fabric is covered.

Crazy Log Cabin – uses wedge shapes and a strange center shape, it is great for using up left-over scraps.

Pineapple Log Cabin – logs are added on the corners as well as parallel to the foundation edges

See foundation method instructions on page 18.

◂ log cabin: chain-piecing method, courthouse steps layout

By using eight colors for the logs, plus black in the center, and turning alternate units by 90° you get wonderful rainbow diamonds happening. Just imagine them repeated across a whole quilt!

See Log Cabin Chain Piecing method on page 18.

log cabin: regular, folded, piped method ▸

Here regular-width black piping is added to each colored log in a rotational setting. The colors progress slowly through the color wheel and the piping is folded inwards.
See Log Cabin Piped Method instructions page 19.

log cabin: irregular, folded, piped method ▸

In this example, irregular widths of colored piping are inserted between black logs. The colors in the piping progress slowly around the color wheel and the piping faces outwards.
See Log Cabin Piped Method instructions page 19.

cathedral window ▸

In Cathedral Window, you fold the four corners of a square of fabric into the center, then repeat with the new set of four corners and tack in place. Several units are joined along the square edges by overcasting on the back—or on front if you want it to be reversible. Smaller squares of colored fabric are laid across the joins on point to form the 'panes', then the diagonal folded edges of the original square are pulled back and rolled to cover the raw edges of the 'panes' and secured with appliqué or running stitch. In Secret Garden, you put another square of fabric underneath the last set of folded points before appliquéing the top square down.

◂ cathedral spire

This is simply Cathedral Window but based on a rectangular base rather than a square one.
Distorted Cathedral Window uses a mixture of square and rectangular based blocks to create stunning optical effects. Hexagonal shapes or virtually any other symmetrical shape which tessellates can be used, but you need to know how to draft the original starting shape.

◂ chinese coin

In the Chinese appliqué method, small squares of fabric are folded corners to center once; then tacked down, butting up next to each other, onto a background fabric of another color. Smaller squares of other colors are placed on top of the first squares, then the folded edges are rolled back and stitched down right through to the background fabric. Because the edges of the first squares are not turned under, the place where the four points meet can look a bit untidy so can be covered with a small circle of felt, or some other small round object like a button or bead.
See carrying cloth on p12.

◂ japanese folded patchwork circle-and-square method

In this technique you cut a square of fabric, plus a circle in a contrasting color slightly larger all around than your square. After folding a hem around the circle it is laid wrong side up, with a square of batting then the square of fabric right side up centered on top, matching the straight of grains. The edges of the circle are pinned over the square and secured with a small quilting/running stitch through all layers. The units are joined with ladder stitch, (or overcast if the back will not be seen). Experiment with circles made from checkerboard and striped patchwork or printed designs - see the center diagonal row here.

japanese folded patchwork two-circle method ▸

Make a cardboard template to the size of square you want. Cut two circles in different colors slightly larger than the square. Sew around the circles, right sides together, leaving a short gap near the straight of grain to turn through. Turn right side out and press. Fold all the sides in around the template, trying to follow the straight of grain. Press the folds and remove the template, then appliqué the edges down, or do a running stitch as shown here.

spanish points ▸

Although these are traditionally cut on the bias, it is more economical to cut on the straight of grain. Cut rectangular strips, and with wrong side facing fold up a seam allowance on the bottom long side. Mark the center of the folded side and fold up one bottom corner, then the other so they overlap and an equilateral triangle appears, pointing downwards. Pin one row with raw edge tips touching and then go back on the same row filling in the gaps. Sew in place and then move on to the next row.

somerset or quill patchwork ▸

Take a small rectangle of fabric and turn up a fold along the bottom long edge. Fold the tips of the folded edge in to the center, to create a triangle with a slit down the middle. These can be set in rounds, as shown here in Jean Martin's cushion, or set into seams for decoration. You can also start with a square folded in half—this is more wasteful and heavier on bigger objects, but there is less risk of raw edges being exposed.

basic techniques

All the blocks in this section are based on a 10in (25cm) finished square

LOG CABIN: FOUNDATION METHOD, SUNSHINE AND SHADOW LAYOUT

1 Start with a 10½ x 10½in (26.5 x 26.5cm) piece of white base fabric. Fold and press the base fabric diagonally both ways. Place a 2½in (6.5cm) square of black fabric in the center and lay out 1½in (4cm) strips of colored fabric in the order you wish them to appear. For Sunshine and Shadow, light colors go on one side and dark colors on the other side.

2 Lay the first color wrong side down on one edge of the black square. Stitch with a short straight stitch and ¼in (6mm) seam.

3 At the end, lift the presser foot and move the block so you can cut the strip to length parallel to the edge of the square and unfold it.

4 Lay the second strip along the end of the first strip and the next side of the square. Stitch to the end.

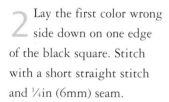

5 Do two sides of a light color and then two sides of the dark. Continue until the white backing fabric is covered.

LOG CABIN: CHAIN PIECING METHOD, COURTHOUSE STEPS LAYOUT

1 Cut four 1½in (4cm) squares of black fabric. Cut two 1in (2.5cm) wide strips of each color you want to use. Lay the first 1in (2.5cm) wide strip on the machine, with the four black squares in a row on top.

2 Stitch in position with ¼in (6mm) seam. Cut the strip at the end of the squares. Repeat, adding the second strip of the same color to the opposite side.

3 Cut the units apart and press the seams open.

4 Lay the units on the second color strip, with right sides together. Chain stitch all four units.

5 Stitch the other side of each unit to the second strip. Cut the units apart and press. Continue until there are four colors each side of the square.

6 Turn two units 90° and join units together, then join the other two. When you join the pairs together all eight colors should run in

LOG CABIN: PIPED METHOD

1 For a black background and narrow, colored piping, start with a 2½in (6.5cm) black square. Fold 1in (2.5cm) colored piping in half and add to one edge, with a ³⁄₁₆in (4.5mm) seam.

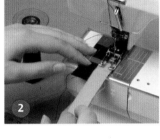

2 Add a 1½in (4cm) black 'log' with ¼in (6mm) seam. Turn the unit 90° and add a second length of colored piping.

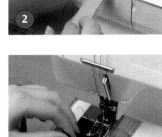

3 Add the second black log strip. In the photograph the unit has been turned right side down onto the strip—this just makes it a little bit easier to see how far to sew.

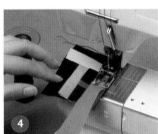

4 Continue adding piping and strips till the block is 10in (25cm) square. Be careful to keep adding the logs in the same direction (counterclockwise).

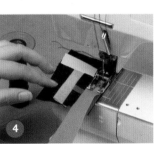

5 The finished piece has a black background with colored folded strips.

Options
- use wider piping
- use colored background and black piping
- let the piping face inwards
- let the piping face outwards
- use a variety of widths of piping

order in a diamond shape. This sample shows Courthouse Steps layout, but you can change color and block layout to achieve different effects.

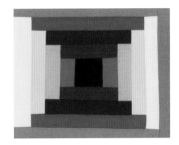

LOG CABIN: FOLDED METHOD

1 Cut your strips twice the width you want them, plus seam allowances. Start with a square on a base fabric as in the foundation method log cabin on page 18. Fold the strips in half and add them around the square in Sunshine and Shadow layout.

2 This sample shows the strips added around in a spiral layout.

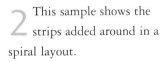

> **TIP**
> *Chain piecing is a very quick method if you are making lots of units the same.*

FLAT PIPING—TRADITIONAL METHOD

1 For a black background with colored tucks cut 10½ x 1½in (26.5 x 4cm) strips of fabric, nine in colors and ten in black.

2 For black piping with a colored background cut 10½ x 1½in (26.5 x 4cm) strips of fabric, ten in colors and nine in black.

3 Join one folded strip of piping to each background strip with a 3/16in (4.5mm) seam. Chain piece them in the order they will end up—there should be one background strip left over.

4 Cut the units apart. Take the first two strips and join with a ¼in (6mm) seam, then sew each following pair together. The photo shows the second strip without its piping on.

5 Join two units together into fours. Join everything together into a square including the remaining backing strip.

FLAT PIPING—LOUISE'S METHOD

1 This is a great way to use up lots of odd leftover strips of varying widths—the photo shows a sample with uneven widths in both backing and piping.

2 Join lots of 10½in (26.5cm) long strips of fabric together with a 3/16in (4.5mm) seam, alternating black with a sequence of bright colors.

3 When you have your flat fabric you can decide where the tucks will be— either in the black or in the colored strips.

4 When you have decided whether you want black tucks or colored tucks, join the two adjacent seams together to make them, using a ¼in (6mm) seam.

> **TIP**
> *See Caryl Bryer Fallert's book A Spectrum of Quilts 1983–1995 for fantastic quilts in the traditional technique.*

MANIPULATION

You can fold on the seam line, or change the tuck sequence partway along a panel. You can then manipulate the piping (tucks) in an enormous variety of ways.

WAVE TUCKS

Press all the seams the same direction. Stitch all folds down at the each edge of the block (just inside the seam allowance) in the direction that they are lying. Mark a line down the center of the block, at 90° to the tucks, then stitch along it, again in the direction the tucks are lying. Mark lines midway between the three sewn lines. Twist each tuck and the seams underneath in the opposite direction, then stitch along the new lines to hold them down in this direction. This will create a series of waves, with the tucks pointing in one direction, then the other.

TWIST TUCKS

Press all the seams the same direction. Stitch the folds down along one edge of the block (just inside the seam allowance) in the direction that they are lying. Fold the other end of the tucks back the other way so there is a twist in the middle of each, then stitch down.

Detail of a twist tuck on the Twist and Grout cushion - see page 90.

preparation — wendy's base

Although this book is about folding fabric, I recommend that you practice the folding techniques in paper first. It is important that you work with perfect squares, so buy a pack of origami paper or cut some squares from a pad of cheap drawing paper. To do this, tear off the top sheet and place it at right angles over the next one, lining up the top left hand corners. Place a metal ruler along the right-hand side and cut with a craft knife. In this way you can cut several sheets at once. You can use the narrow strips left over for telephone messages or shopping lists. For some of your experiments, it is worth drawing stitches or a colored line around the edge of both sides of the paper before you start folding, because the outside edge of the square can become an intricate pattern in the middle, once it is folded.

When you do start using fabrics, you will find that some are much easier to fold than others. The best fabric by far is 100% pure cotton, as it retains the creases well and doesn't fray too much. For small squares, a fine cotton is needed, such as lawn, organdy, muslin, scrim, or sheeting. For larger squares, a thicker fabric can be used, such as quilters-weight cotton, denim, heavier muslin or stiffened linen. For very crisp folds and for 3D effects, use spray starch while you are pressing in the folds.

Other types of thinner fabrics, like polycottons, can be used if they are bonded together, as the fusible webbing slightly stiffens the fabric and prevents fraying. This is also the perfect way to get a double-sided fabric with a different color on each side. Many origami patterns show both sides at the same time. Two thick fabrics bonded together will be too bulky to fold accurately but you can bond one thicker fabric to a very thin one. Even chiffon will change the color of one side.

PREPARING A DOUBLE-SIDED SQUARE OF FABRIC

1 First cut a square from fusible webbing—it should be slightly larger than four times the size of the finished folded square (twice the width and twice the length.) Place the square web-side down onto one of your chosen fabrics, keeping the sides as near as possible to the same direction as the weave of the fabric, then press it down.

2 Remove the backing paper. Do not throw away this square of paper as you can use it to experiment with folding semi-transparent material.

3 Press the square down onto the other color fabric, still keeping to the direction of the weave.

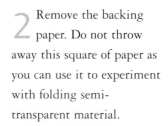

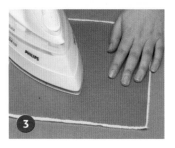

4 The easiest way to cut out a perfect square is to use a commercial plastic ruler. If the ruler is very smooth, you can put self-adhesive spots of sandpaper on the back to prevent it from slipping on the fabric.

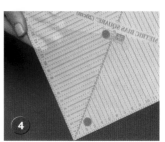

5 Whichever ruler or template you use, place it in the center of your fabric and cut around the square with a rotary cutter.

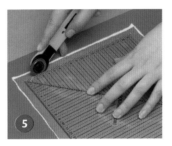

6 If the edge is going to be a feature of the finished pattern, machine stitch, using a close zigzag, all around the four sides with a decorative thread.

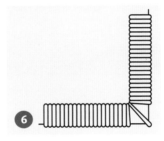

Do not start at a corner, but part way down one side, so when you have stitched all around the square you can over-run by ¼in (6mm) and trim off the ends. As you approach the first corner, slow down and stop one stitch-width away from the corner, with the needle in the fabric. Lift the presser foot and half turn the fabric. Lower the presser foot; do one stitch across the corner and as the needle is returning, give the fabric a tiny hitch so that the needle returns to the same spot as the last stitch. Lift the presser foot again; complete the turn; lower the presser foot and continue stitching down the next side. Repeat on all corners.

wendy's base

This is an ancient origami base, sometimes called a windmill base and sometimes a boat base in origami books. By trial and error, over the last 14 years, I have developed the best way to fold it in fabric.

1 Find the center of the square by folding the opposite corners together, and press the diagonal creases. These creases will act as guidelines in some of the later folding patterns. If you do not want complete diagonal lines showing, just press the small area where the lines cross in the middle.

2 Fold the corners to the central point—in origami terms this is called a blintz-fold. With fabric, the best way to do this is to take two adjacent corners to the center together and only press half of each side to the point.

3 Take one corner and the next together and so on until you get to the last and the first again, to complete the pressing of each side.

4 Unfold again and TURN THE SQUARE OVER. Fold all four sides to the center, one at a time. Unfold the previous crease before doing the next. To make sure this fold is straight, line up the corners with the points where the blintz creases meet and through the center point.

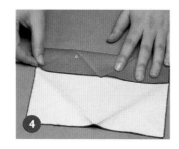

5 When you press this crease, do it carefully in three parts so that you avoid pressing out the blintz creases on the other side. This is your pattern of pre-creasing.

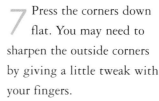

6 With the thumb and forefinger of each hand, lift up the center point of each side and move them to the center—the whole square will collapse in on itself.

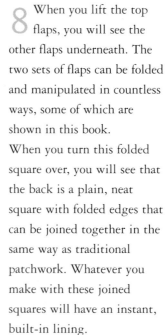

7 Press the corners down flat. You may need to sharpen the outside corners by giving a little tweak with your fingers.

8 When you lift the top flaps, you will see the other flaps underneath. The two sets of flaps can be folded and manipulated in countless ways, some of which are shown in this book.
When you turn this folded square over, you will see that the back is a plain, neat square with folded edges that can be joined together in the same way as traditional patchwork. Whatever you make with these joined squares will have an instant, built-in lining.

positive negative

I was once invited to demonstrate my origami techniques in fabric at a Homemakers' Event in one of London's Oxford Street department stores. I thought that it would be appropriate to use some fabric that was likely to be used in the home. Looking through a selection of curtain fabrics, I noticed that many of the two-color patterns were woven in such a way that the back was a negative of the front and so a different color was dominant on each side. This would be ideal, I thought, to make some origami-style cushion covers to match the curtains. So, next time you have to buy fabric for new curtains, bear this in mind. The following method uses the simplest ways of folding the two layers of flaps created in Wendy's Base.

Project by Wendy Lowes   *Size: 18 x 18in (45 x 45cm)*

MATERIALS:

FRONT AND BACK:

❖ 2yds (180cm) of 54in (134cm) wide double-sided
   fabric, such as double-cloth upholstery fabric
❖ Matching thread for edging and joining squares

INSIDE:

❖ 18in (45cm) square pillow form

COLOR LAYOUT

Sew the blocks together alternately to achieve a checker-board effect with the different blocks.

instructions ▶

1 Cut nine 12in (30cm) squares and nine 4½in (11cm) squares from the fabric, using one of the cutting methods illustrated on page 22. If there is an obvious pattern, try to show it evenly within each square.

2 Machine zig-zag satin stitch around the edges of the large squares. (See page 23.)

3 Fold each of the large squares into Wendy's Base. (See page 24.) Fold five squares with the darker color on the outside and four squares with the lighter color on the outside.

4 Press the folds firmly with an iron, then unfold again. The creases should show clearly.

5 Fold the corners in to where the creases cross each other.

6 Place one of the smaller squares, opposite color side up, in the middle of the large square.

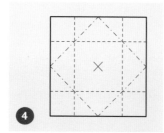

TIP
- *The color which is facing you when you start to fold in step 3 will end up on the outside.*

7 Re-fold on the basic fold creases.

8 Press the inner folded flaps back to about ½in (1.5cm) away from the outer folds. Use a few holding stitches to fix the corners of these inner triangles which will also hold in place the inserted smaller square of fabric.

9 Join alternately dark and light blocks together, using small overcast stitches at the back. This will give you a checkerboard pattern.

10 To make the back of the cushion cover, cut two pieces of fabric, one 6 x 18in (15 x 45cm) and the other one 17½ x 18in (44.5 x 45cm).

11 Turn under ½in (1.5cm), then ½in (1.5cm) again, along one 18in (45cm) edge of each piece. Press the hem.

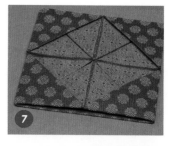

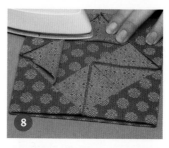

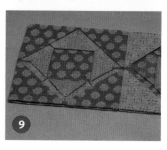

The folds create a wonderful interplay of light and color across the three-dimensional surface of the cushion.

12 Overlap the turned-under edges of the two pieces by 2½in (6.5cm) with the smaller piece underneath on the right side. Pin together at the sides to hold in place. Neaten all the cut edges with a zig-zag machine stitch, which will also hold the overlapping edges together at the sides.

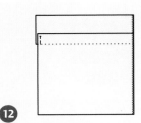

13 Carefully place these two overlapping pieces face down on the front of the cushion cover.

14 Turn over; fold back the edges all around so that the back is exactly the same size as the front.

TIP

- If you find that the opening in the back of the cushion is too loose, you can add a few snaps or Velcro spots to keep it closed.

15 Miter the corners of the turned edges. First fold the corner at 45°.

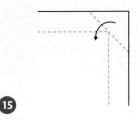

16 Fold down each side as shown.

17 Stitch along the miter line.

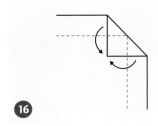

18 Pin the front and the back together with the right sides facing. Join together by stitching all round the outside edge with small overcast stitches.

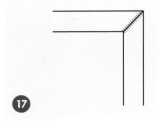

19 Turn the cover to the right side through the opening across the back. Use the same opening to insert the pillow form.

the pattern unfolds

While playing about with my computer, I discovered some interesting little patterns in the section called Clipart. I chose a few of the simplest black and white geometric motifs and printed them out as 6in (15cm) squares. After cutting them out, I experimented with folding them in various different ways and got quite excited at how they began to form new patterns. When several were joined as in a patchwork, even more patterns began to emerge. I transfered the patterns onto a silk-screen, then printed them twenty-five times onto white cotton sheeting. If you do not have access to silk-screen equipment, it would be just as effective to print these very simple, basic patterns by using a stencil or freezer paper.

The twenty-five folded pieces for this hanging were originally intended to become a cushion, but when they were laid out on the table ready for sewing, they looked much more interesting unsewn. I decided to make them into a diamond-shaped hanging, with the top two outside rows completely stitched down and each row after that with some of the inner flaps left unsewn. The three pieces at the bottom corner were only half sewn, so that nearly all the flaps unfolded and revealed the original pattern printed onto the fabric.

Project by Wendy Lowes *Size: 21 x 21in (52.5 x 57.5cm)*

MATERIALS:

❖ 1yd (90cm) of 42in (105cm) wide white cotton fabric, pre-washed
❖ Freezer paper, craft knife and ruler to cut stencils
❖ Baking parchment
❖ Black permanent fabric paint and small sponge
❖ White and black threads for joining the folded squares
❖ Two thin hanging rods

BLOCK LAYOUT

Block 1 is completely folded and stitched.
Block 2 has one flap unfolded.
Block 3 has two flaps unfolded.
Block 4 has three flaps unfolded.
The bottom corner block is completely unfolded.

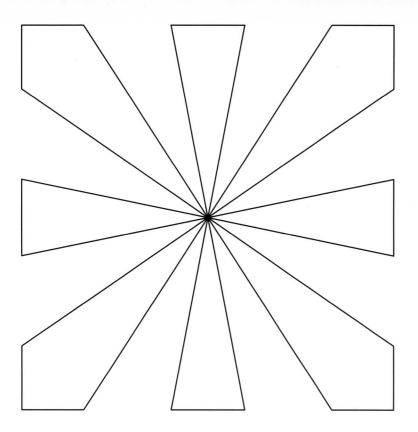

instructions ▸

1 Enlarge the template above by 150%, to 6in (15cm) square. Cut a 6½in (16.5cm) square of freezer paper and trace the template. Using a craft knife and ruler, cut out the shapes. Cut the white fabric into 25 squares, each 6½in (16.5cm).

2 Iron the cut-out freezer paper stencil onto one of the fabric squares. Place on top of a piece of baking parchment and tape the edges to hold in place. Wearing rubber gloves to protect your hands, dip the sponge into the black fabric paint and dab evenly in the cut spaces.

3 When the paint is dry, remove the stencil and set the paint according to the manufacturer's instructions.

4 With a hot iron, turn under a ¼in (6mm) border. You now have a 6in (15cm) printed square ready for folding.

5 Still using the iron, fold the square to Wendy's Base (see page 24). Start the blintz folds with the printed side down, so the collapsed square will have the folded-under edge showing on the top. Repeat the sequence on all 25 squares.

6 Fold the top flaps back to the outside corners.

7 Fold all four of the inside flaps back so that the points are about ¼in (6mm) away from the outside edge. Sew in place with two or three holding stitches.

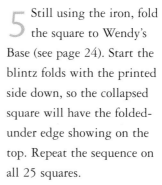

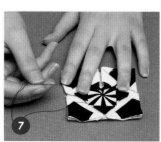

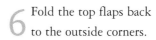

8 Repeat on another nine squares, so there are ten blocks with all four flaps folded and stitched in place.

9 On six of the squares, fold back and stitch three of the inside flaps.

10 On three squares, fold back and stitch two adjacent inside flaps.

11 On two of the squares, fold back and stitch one of the inside flaps. On the remaining four squares, leave the inside flaps down.

12 Using ladder stitch, join the blocks together following the layout on page 30. Leave out the bottom square at this stage. Make sure you catch the folded-under edges together. Use black thread where the pattern is black and white thread where it is white.

The blocks in the top V-shape row have all four inside flaps turned back. On the outside edge, hem the top flaps to the folded edge underneath.

The top block in the second V-shaped row is completely stitched. The three blocks on each side have one inner flap left loose.

The third V-shaped row has two adjacent inner flaps left loose on the top block and on the blocks on either

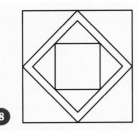

8

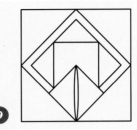

9

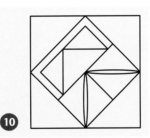

10

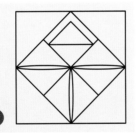

11

side. The outer blocks on each side have three inner flaps left loose.

On the fourth row, the top block has all four inner flaps left loose. The other block on each side will be joined on the top two sides only, with the rest of the block (inner and outer flaps) left loose.

The bottom block is completely unfolded. It fits into the last space with the top two sides each stitched to one of the unfolded sides from the previous row. See diagram and detail photo of bottom of hanging.

13 Using small loops of white tape, attach two thin rods at the back of the hanging, one at the widest point and one about 4in (10cm) from the top. Attach a hanging loop of wire or thread to the top rod.

The printed shapes change depending on how the square of fabric is folded, creating even more intricate patterns.

denim windmills

This is a very good project to make if you have young children at home who like sitting on the floor! Denim is popular with young people and is an ideal fabric for origami techniques as it already has a different color on the reverse side. It is also hard-wearing and washable.

The method of folding used in this project hides all of the raw edges of the squares, which is particularly good for something like a floorcushion, which will need regular laundering. It also protects the edges from fraying during the rough and tumble of family life.

Project by Wendy Lowes   *Size: 24 x 24in (60 x 60cm)*

MATERIALS:
❖ 2¾yds (247.5cm) of 42in (105cm) wide denim, cut into:
  16 pieces each 12in (30cm) square
  1 piece 8 x 24⅜in (20 x 61.5cm)
  1 piece 23 x 24⅜in (57.5 x 61.5cm)
❖ Matching thread for joining squares
❖ Thicker thread for top-stitching
❖ 16 buttons for the centers of the squares
❖ 24in (60cm) square pillow form

COLOR LAYOUT
The two colors come from the two sides of the denim. This is a simple project to piece, as all the blocks are identical.

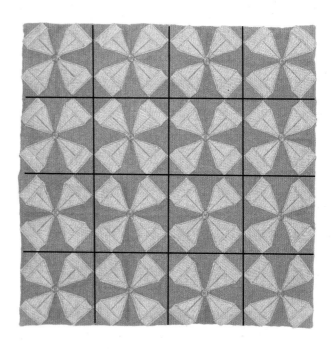

instructions ▸

1 Fold each square to Wendy's Base (see page 24) so that the darker color shows on the outside.

2 Fold the four top flaps right back to the corners —you will now see only the lighter color.

3 Press firmly with an iron —a steam iron, if you have one.

4 Unfold; then fold the corners of the flaps up to the centers of the crease lines that you have just made.

5 Then fold back the first creases with the folded corners underneath.

6 The darker color will now show at the corners of the square.

7 Lift one of the flaps sideways.

8 Fold behind to the center of the diagonal.

9 Press the turned-under flap down.

10 Repeat on all eight side flaps.

11 There will still be some small raw edges in the middle. To hide these, just fold under from the center of the square to the edge of the first fold on all eight side flaps.

12 Top-stitch as shown in the diagram.

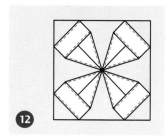

13 There will probably be a few loose strands in the very middle of the square, where the points meet; you can sew a button there to hide them.

14 Join the blocks together in four rows of four. Use an overcast stitch at the back but make sure that all the front edges are joined.

15 Turn under ½in (1.5cm), then ½in (1.5cm) again, along one 24in (60cm) edge of each piece. Press the hem. Make the back of the cushion by the same method as described for the Positive-Negative Cushion, steps 10-17, on page 28.

A detail of the cushion, showing the windmill shape and the button in the center of the square.

TIP

- If you want to make an even bigger floor-cushion, get enough denim for 25 squares plus 36in (90cm) for the back.
- If the denim you are using frays easily, seal the edges with an anti-fraying adhesive.
- You will need a very sharp needle and a thimble.

enigma variations

This is a 36in (90cm) square sampler quilt showing several folding variations from a basic module, which I have called a Flower-wheel. It is a very ancient Japanese origami module which is usually part of a *kusudama*, a six-sided, decorative ball. In his book on Kusudamas, Makoto Yamaguchi calls it a Diamond, I suppose because it resembles the facets of a cut diamond. In her book on the same subject, Tomoko Fuse calls it a Chrysanthemum. I have called it a Flower-wheel because the satin-stitched edges of the fabric square, when folded, look like the spokes of a wheel in the middle of an octagon of triangular petals. This quilt also shows that, if you put square patches over the joins between the folded blocks, tucked under the top layer of folds, some very interesting shapes appear. In a normal, flat quilt these shapes would involve very intricate cutting and piecing.

Project by Wendy Lowes   *Size: 36 x 36in (90 x 90cm)*

MATERIALS:
YARDAGE IS BASED ON 42-IN (105CM) WIDE COTTON FABRIC:
- ❖ 3¼yds (292.5cm) of white, cut into 69 squares, 8in (20cm) each
- ❖ 2yds (180cm) of dark orange, cut into 41 squares, 8in (20cm) each
- ❖ 1½yds (135cm) of light orange, cut into 28 squares, 8in (20cm) each
- ❖ 1⅞yds (169cm) of turquoise, cut into:
  12 squares, 5½in (14cm) each
  24 squares, 4½in (11.5cm) each
  96 squares, 2¾in (7cm) each
- ❖ ⅜yd (34cm) of navy blue, cut into 41 squares, 2¾in (7cm) each
- ❖ 15½yds (1395cm) of 12-in (30cm) wide fusible webbing, cut into 69 squares, 8ins (20cm) each and 120 squares, 2¾in (7cm) each
- ❖ Approximately 12 x 16in (30 x 40cm) lightweight batting, cut into 12 squares, 3¾in (9.5cm) each
- ❖ Matching thread for joining squares
- ❖ Navy blue thread for edging squares
- ❖ Turquoise blue thread for quilting

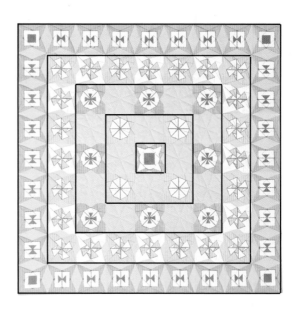

COLOR LAYOUT
Center square – dark orange/white.
Row 1 – alternate light orange/white & blue bagged squares.
Row 2 – alternate dark orange/white & blue bagged squares.
Inner Border – light orange/white with alternate outer color.
Outer Border – dark orange/white.
All squares have turquoise patches over joins and under folds.

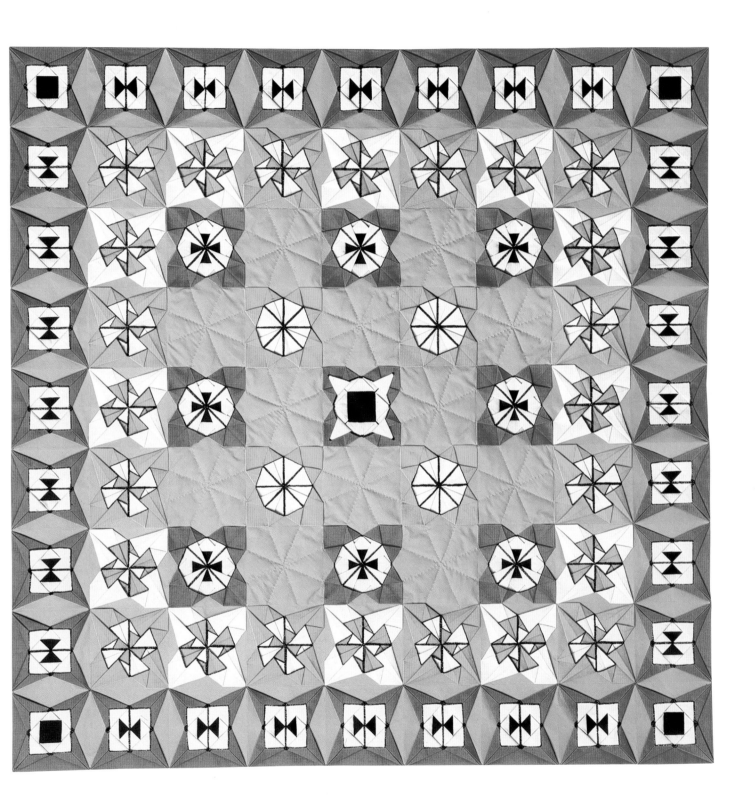

instructions ▸

CENTRAL PANEL:

1 Using the larger squares of fusible webbing and the method shown on page 22, back the 41 squares of dark orange and 28 squares of light orange with white.

2 With navy blue thread, machine satin-stitch around the edges of the squares, as shown on page 23.

3 For the basic flower-wheel blocks, take nine dark orange/white squares and four light orange/white squares and fold as Wendy's Base (See page 24) with the orange color on the outside.

4 Fold in the double edges of the flaps to the diagonal crease lines, so that the points meet in the center. Pin in place.

5 Open up these double edges, using the tip of your finger, and squash-fold the wide end down into a little triangular shape.

6 Press firmly. When all eight flaps have been opened up in this way, the flower-wheel shape appears.

7 On the four light orange/white blocks, slip stitch the open edges of the 'spokes' together, using the same navy blue thread as the edging.

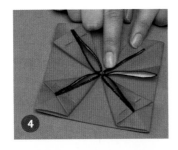

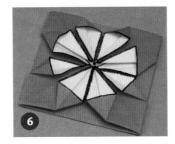

TIP
- *All of the folded squares in this project are fused double-sided fabric.*
- *Use a steam-iron to press the shapes; it will make the creases sharper.*

DO NOT STITCH THROUGH TO THE LOWER LAYER; later, the turquoise patches will tuck under these folds.

8 Using the twenty-four 4½in (11.5cm) squares of turquoise fabric, make twelve 4in (10cm) bagged squares, as shown on page 78, steps 1–6. Before you close the opening in each bag, insert a 3¾in (9.5cm) square of batting with the tips of all four corners chopped off.

9 Start to assemble the center of the quilt, joining the squares with ladder stitch in five rows of five units, following the color layout on page 38. This is how they will look on the back.

10 This is how they will look on the front.

11 Take twenty-four of the 2¾in (7cm) squares of fusible webbing and cut them in half diagonally, to make 48 triangles. Iron down a triangular piece of webbing on each corner of all twelve 5½in (14cm) squares of turquoise, then carefully peel off the backing paper.

12 Snip off a small piece of the corners.

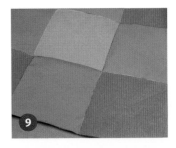

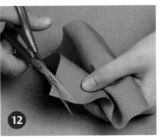

13 Place these squares (webbing side down) on point over the turquoise squares, tucking the webbed corners under the folds of the adjacent units.

14 Iron the corners to bond them in place. Using a quilter's mini-iron would make this process much easier.

15 This is the rather attractive eight-point star shape that is formed by this process.

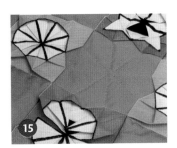

16 Using a Hera marker or the point of a knitting needle and a ruler, mark lines across the star shape. With a quilting needle and matching thread, sew tiny stab stitches along the marked lines. For the time being, just quilt the four central stars.

When all the star patches are in place, the webbed corners protruding from the outer edge of the panel will be unattached, waiting for the next rows of units.

For clarity, the following pictures will show the treatment of individual squares not in the quilt.

17 In each of the nine dark orange/white blocks, open up all the folds, place a 2¾in (7cm) square of navy blue fabric in the center, and re-fold the blocks.

18 Fold back the top four flaps as far as possible, and pin in place.

19 Fold back the points of the inner four flaps to the edge of the white circle. Pin to hold in place. After the turquoise pieces have been inserted (see page 42, step 9) you can stitch the flaps in place with navy thread.

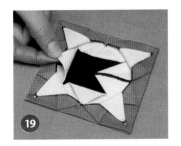

20 In the central square only, use holding stitches to secure the points of the top four flaps in the same position as in step 18.

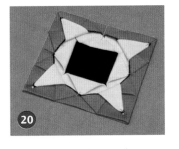

21 In the other eight dark orange/white blocks, un-pin the top four flaps and put them back in their original position.

Slip-stitch the open navy blue edges together with matching thread and hold the four points together with a cross stitch in the center.

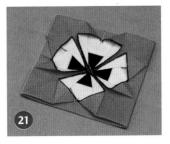

22 On all 13 of the completed blocks, use matching light or dark orange thread to put a holding stitch at the tip of each triangular petal, after the blue patches have been inserted between the blocks.

INNER BORDER:

1 Take the 24 remaining light orange/white squares and fold them to Wendy's Base; twelve with orange on the outside and twelve with white on the outside.

2 On each of the top flaps, fold the double edges, on the right-hand sides only, to the diagonal crease lines, with the points in the center. Open the wide ends with the tip of your finger and squash fold the little triangles, as before. Press firmly.

3 Fold the double edges on the left-hand sides of the flaps, from the outer corners of the square, so that the wide ends overlap the flaps on the right-hand sides.

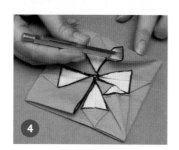

4 Lift and, using a narrow pointed implement, squash fold these longer, narrower triangles.

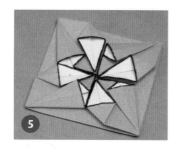

5 The small white triangles at the wide ends will lie neatly between the flaps on the right-hand sides.

6 Hold down the points in the middle with a cross stitch.

7 Use ladder stitch to join the folded blocks together in four strips,

alternating the outside colors, and following the layout on page 38.

8 The rest of the star patches can now be quilted, as in step 16 on page 41.

9 Take 36 of the 2¾in (7cm) squares of turquoise fabric and back them with fusible webbing. Peel off the backing paper; snip a bit off two opposite corners of each patch. Iron 12 of the blue patches, on point, between the new rows of folded blocks and the folded blocks at the outer edge of the central panel, tucking the snipped corners under the folds. In the same way, iron 24 blue patches between the white and pale orange blocks. These will create rather interesting lightning shapes between the blocks.

OUTER BORDER:

1 Take the remaining 32 dark orange/ white squares. Fold to Wendy's Base, all with the dark orange on the outside.

2 Open up the folds and place squares of the navy blue fabric inside as in step 17 on page 41, then re-fold the blocks.

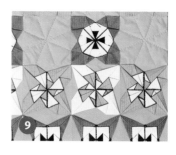

3 Fold in the double edges of the flaps to the diagonal crease lines, so that the points are at the outside corners of the squares. Press firmly.

4 At each corner, hold the edges of the folded flaps together, while turning back the small triangle from the center of the square, revealing the white underneath. Pin the triangle in place.

With the navy blue thread, make a few stitches to hold down the point of the folded-back triangle, which also holds the two folded edges together.

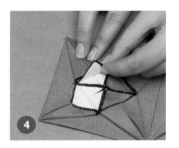

5 Use ladder stitch to join the folded blocks together in four strips, two strips of nine blocks and two strips of seven blocks.

Join the strips of seven blocks to opposite sides of the existing quilt; then join the strips of nine blocks to the other two sides of the existing quilt.

6 Take 60 of the 2¾in (7cm) squares of turquoise fabric and back them with fusible webbing. Peel off the backing paper and snip a bit off two opposite corners of each patch. Place them on point over the joins between the blocks, tucking the snipped

TIP
- *Sometimes, when I am teaching the flower-wheel, someone in the class will accidentally fold the edges of the flaps to the diagonal creases with the points at the outside corners of the square instead of the middle. I always say that it is not a mistake; just a variation! This variation is used for the outside border rows of the quilt.*

corners under the folds on each side; press. Thirty-two will go between the blocks of the outer border and 28 will go between the blocks of the outer border row and the inner border row.

7 In each block of the outer border, fold back two of the opposite inner flaps in the same direction as the row.

8 Stitch down the points with holding stitches. This will reveal a little navy blue butterfly shape in the center.

9 In the four outer corner blocks only, fold and stitch all the inner flaps back, revealing navy blue squares.

10 In the butterfly blocks, slip-stitch the navy blue edges together between the 'wings', securing both ends of the join through all layers. The quilt is now complete.

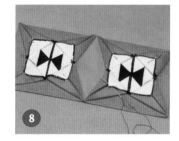

light fantastic

After putting fusible webbing onto squares of fabric in some of the earlier projects, I peeled off the backing paper but did not throw it away. Here were some squares of semi-transparent paper that invited experimental folding and I discovered that these folded squares, when held up to the light, showed the layers underneath as different tones. Of course, I wanted to get this same effect in folded fabric and found that pure cotton organdy was perfect for this because it is very crisp and holds creases really well even without using an iron. Synthetic organza does not work in the same way because it is too slippery.

This little hanging was really an experiment, but a bigger one could be used in a window instead of a sheer curtain. Hanging against a dark background, a different effect is obtained. Organdy can be obtained in black, white and several pastel colors—I used cream.

Project by Wendy Lowes   *Size: 20 x 20in (50 x 50cm)*

MATERIALS:
❖ ¾yd (68cm) of 45in (115cm) wide cotton organdy, cut into 25 squares, 8in (20cm) each
❖ Gold metallic machine-embroidery thread for edging.
❖ Invisible nylon thread for joining
❖ Two 20in (50cm) lengths of clear narrow acrylic rod for hanging

BLOCK LAYOUT
The blocks are joined in rows of five, sewing all the folded-back corners together with invisible nylon thread.

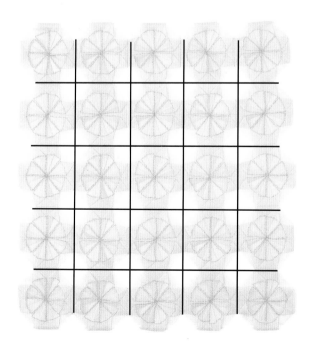

instructions ▶

1 Using the gold thread, sew around all the squares of organdy with close zig-zag machine stitching, as shown in the instructions on page 23.

2 Fold all the squares to Wendy's Base, as shown on page 24.

3 Continue folding each square into the flower-wheel unit, as shown in steps 4–6 on page 40.

4 Using the same gold thread as for the edging, slip-stitch the open edges together on all the 'spokes'. Do this on the underneath flaps first, then on the top flaps. Join the points together with a cross stitch.

5 Fold back the corners of the folded squares, between the outer points of the triangular petals. This will create an octagon shape.

6 Join the blocks together in five rows of five, by stitching together the folded corners with a length of invisible nylon thread.

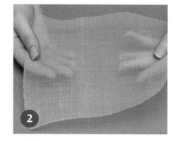

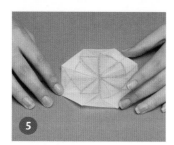

7 On the unjoined outside edges of the hanging, just catch the folded corners at the back, using a few holding stitches.

8 At the top and the bottom of the hanging, slide a narrow acrylic rod through the row of folded-back corners.

9 Tie a short length of thicker nylon thread or thin fishing line to the upper rod for hanging.

TIP
- Other translucent fabrics can be used for this project, as long as they are stiff enough to hold a crisp fold.
- Synthetic fabrics tend to be too slippery to fold into such precise geometric shapes.
- Try alternative folded geometric shapes in translucent paper to come up with your own variations on this project.
- The color of the edge stitching should contrast with the fabric because the edge forms an intricate pattern after the square has been folded.

When this block is made in translucent organdy, it looks very different against dark and light backgrounds.

Under bright lights the gold thread gleams, delineating the shapes within the folded block.

eastern promise

In the introduction at the beginning of this book, I mentioned that origami models of birds, animals, or fish can often be taken out of context and seen as geometric shapes. The base unit for this wall hanging is a perfect example of this. Once, to keep a group of children amused, I made some origami angel-fish in fabric. While playing with these shapes, I was pleased with the effect when I put two angel-fish together, back-to-back. The resulting hanging is also inspired by the colors and geometric shapes in Islamic decorative art.

Project by Wendy Lowes   *Size: 12¼ x 22½ins (30.5 x 56.5cm)*

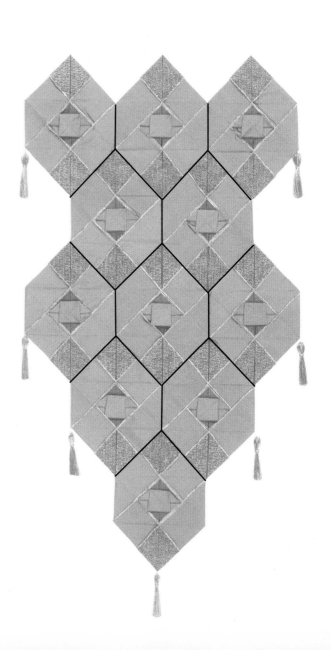

MATERIALS

- ❖ ¾yd (68cm) of 42in (105cm) wide dark blue silk, cut into 22 squares, 6in (15cm) each
- ❖ ¾yd (68cm) of 42in (105cm) wide medium blue silk, cut into 22 squares, 6in (15cm) each
- ❖ 2yds (180cm) of 12in (30cm) wide fusible webbing, cut into 22 squares, 6in (15cm) each
- ❖ Metallic thread for surface decoration, edging and tassels

COLOR LAYOUT

Choose two colors of silk that go well together. Each block will have both colors showing, making further geometric patterns within the hexagon shape.

instructions ▸

1 Take a square of medium blue and one of dark blue silk and bond them together back to back, wrong sides together, using the method shown on page 22. Repeat with all the other squares; this will give you 22 squares of double-sided silk.

2 Using the metallic thread, machine satin stitch round the edges of each square, as shown on page 23.

3 Pre-crease the squares to Wendy's Base (see page 24) with the lighter color on the outside in each case.

4 Unfold and machine stitch a decorative design across one of the corners, from the fold line half way to the point.

5 Fold the embroidered corner back over to the other side.

6 Now start to collapse the square in sequence. First, fold in the two sides next to the folded, embroidered corner.

7 Fold the diagonally-opposite corner to the crease lines.

8 Next, fold in the two sides next to the small folded corner.

9 Instead of squashing the two remaining corners flat, bring them down to lie beside the small folded corner, like wings. This completes one unit.

10 Using the same metallic thread, make a small cross stitch in the center of the unit, to hold all the folded points together.

11 Take two units and slide them together, with the left-hand wing of one going inside the right-hand wing of the other. The small folded corners will lie on top of each other.

12 Where the wings overlap, use the same metallic thread to hem the satin-stitched edges down, holding the two units together. Some stitching on the back, using thread to match the color of the silk, will also increase stability.

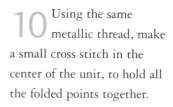

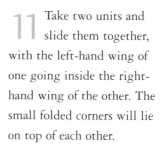

13 Lift the small folded corner in the center of the front. Gently push the forefinger of each hand into the two sides of the folded corner.

14 Squash-fold the center of the block into a small raised square.

15 These blocks can now be joined together with ladder stitch or oversewing at the back. You can join them together as I have done, with little tassels (made from the same metallic thread) hanging from some of the corners, or you could experiment with joining them together in other ways.

TIP
- *If you have a computer and scanner, you can scan one of these units; then clone it on your screen and try out different color schemes and different ways of joining them together.*

The center of each block is a little squashed cushion of folded fabric, which gives a three-dimensional effect.

i never promised you a rose garden

This quilt was originally made for a Quilters' Guild London Area Day Challenge and I was delighted when, under an anonymous voting system, it won joint first prize. The challenge was to make a 24in (60cm) square quilt based on flowers and leaves and the subject was ideal for origami techniques. I had previously made a large three-dimensional hanging in plain, unbleached calico that I called Waterlilies, which had nine sets of four nesting flower shapes. For this smaller quilt, I used similar techniques plus some new ones, but I made it in bright colors.

Project by Wendy Lowes *Size: 24 x 24in (60 x 60cm)*

MATERIALS:

YARDAGE IS BASED ON 42IN (105CM) WIDE COTTON FABRIC

FOR THE OUTER PART OF THE FLOWERS:

❖ ¾yd (68cm) of deep pink fabric, cut into 11 squares, 8in (20cm) each

❖ ¼yd (22.5cm) of medium pink fabric, cut into 5 squares, 8in (20cm) each

FOR THE INNER PART OF THE FLOWERS:

❖ ½yd (45cm) of light-weight red fabric, cut into 7 squares, 8in (20cm) each

❖ ¼yd (22.5cm) of light-weight burgundy fabric, cut into 4 squares, 8in (20cm) each

❖ ¼yd (22.5cm) of pale pink fabric, cut into 5 squares, 8in (20cm) each

❖ Matching threads for edging and sewing down

❖ Some thick, twisted embroidery thread, in a suitable color, to make the centers of the flowers

❖ 4in (10cm) square of lightweight cardboard

FOR THE LEAVES:

❖ ¾yd (68cm) of green fabric, cut into 11 squares, 8in (20cm) each

❖ Matching or contrasting green thread for edging and sewing down

FOR THE BACKGROUND:

❖ ¾yd (68cm) of pale turquoise fabric, cut into one 24½in (61.5cm) square

BACKING:

❖ ¾yd (68cm) of blue fabric, cut into one 24½in (61.5cm) square

❖ Approximately 15 x 22in (37.5 x 55cm) piece of lightweight batting, cut into 24 squares, 3½in (9cm) each

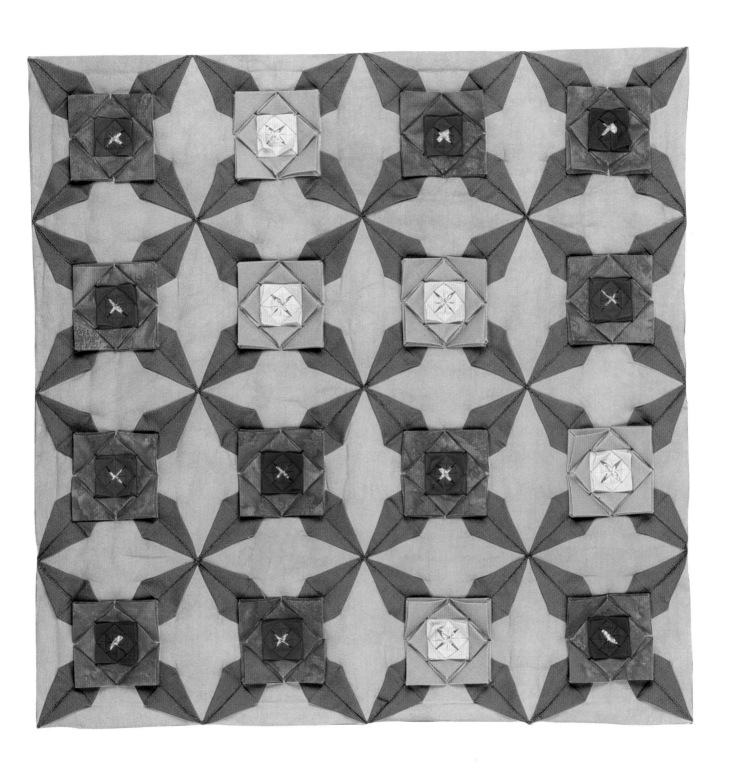

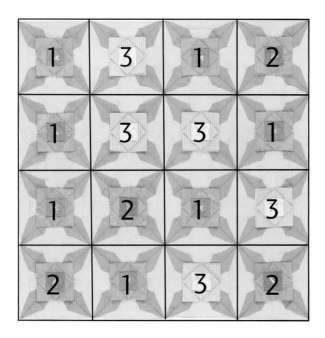

1	3	1	2
1	3	3	1
1	2	1	3
2	1	3	2

COLOR LAYOUT

Make seven flowers with deep pink outer petals and a red center (Block 1). Make four flowers with deep pink outer petals and a burgundy center (Block 2). Make five flowers with medium pink outer petals and pale pink centers (Block 3). Arrange the flowers so that the colors are not symmetrical. Here, the lighter pink flowers form an S-shape swirl through the darker ones.

instructions ▶

OUTER PART OF FLOWERS:

1 Take the 16 larger pink squares, and machine zigzag stitch round the edge of each square using a matching thread. (See instructions on page 23.)

2 Blintz fold the square (see instructions on page 24, step 2) and then put a small piece of sticky tape over the points in the center, to hold them in place.

3 Now fold Wendy's Base from step 1 (see page 24), as if you were starting with a plain square. You will notice that the four top flaps have diagonal openings, but the edges of the flaps are folded.

4 Fold the top flaps back to the point of the outer corners.

5 Press the four corners down firmly.

6 Fold the inner flaps out to the edge and press.

Repeat sequence for all 16 outer flowers.

INNER PART OF FLOWERS:

1 Take the 16 smaller squares and fold under the edges, using a 4in (10cm) square of thin card as a template, as shown in the instructions on page 64.

2 Blintz fold and tape down corners, as described in step 2 for the outer part of flower.

3 Continue to fold in exactly the same way as in step 3 for the outer part of the flower.

4 Now remove the sticky tape from the back and release the four triangular flaps, bringing them out to the side of the inner flower.

5 Place these triangular flaps underneath the inner triangular flaps of the outer flower.

6 Take a short length of the twisted embroidery thread and coil it round your finger a few times. Stitch down in the center of the flower.

Repeat sequence for all 16 inner flowers—the flowers are now complete.

LEAVES:

1 Take the 16 squares of green fabric and machine stitch around the edges as shown on page 23—these edges will become the central veins of the leaves.

2 Fold Wendy's Base (see page 24) making complete diagonal creases in step 1 as a useful guideline.

3 Pick up one of the flaps sideways and fold from the center so the double, stitched edge lies against the diagonal crease mark; press. Fold the other side of the flap to the diagonal crease.

4 Fold the little triangle of the outer corner down over the flaps you have just folded and press firmly.

5 Unfold the last three folds. Pick up the top corner of the flap from inside the last three creases.

6 Pull the flap back on the crease at the outside corner, bringing the stitched edges together.

7 Press firmly. The origami term for this sequence is a 'petal fold.'

8 Repeat on the other three corners.

Repeat on all sets of leaves.

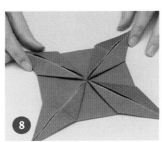

COMBINE FLOWERS AND LEAVES:

1 Remove the sticky tape from the back of the outer flower and release the four triangular flaps, bringing them out to the sides of the flower.

2 Open up the leaf unit from the points in the center and slide the flower unit inside. The point where the lower quarters of two adjacent leaves meet will fit inside the inside flap of the outer flower.

3 Repeat on the three other sides.

4 Secure with holding stitches under the four corners of the flower.

5 With green thread, slip-stitch the exposed part of the machine-stitched edges of the leaves together, down the middle of each leaf.

Repeat sequence for all 16 flowers and leaves units.

ASSEMBLY:

1 Take your background fabric and turn under ¼in (6mm) on all four edges, so that you have a 24in (60cm) square.

2 Make creases as shown in the diagram. The easiest way to do this is to fold in half each way; then in quarters each way; then fold the diagonals across each row of squares.

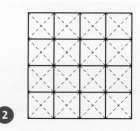

3 At the center of each square, accentuate 6in (15cm) of the diagonal cross with a fabric pencil.

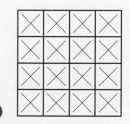

4 Starting with the four middle squares, cut the 6in (15cm) long crosses carefully with sharp scissors.

5 Take one of the flower and leaves units and slot it into one of the cut crosses, tucking the cut edges underneath the leaves and the sides of the flower.

6 The thickened inner flaps of the outer flower are obscuring the inner flower, so they need to be held back by some holding stitches underneath, but not tight enough to make them lie completely flat.

Close-up of one of the flowers, with its pointed petals, the embroidery thread detail just showing in the center.

7 Repeat steps 5 and 6 with the other three central cut crosses. Where the points of four leaves meet in the center of the quilt, stitch them together with a little cross-stitch.

8 Continue to cut the outer rows of crosses and insert the rest of the flowers and leaves in the same way.

9 Turn the whole piece over and you will see the square parts of the leaf units at the back. Place the small squares of batting between these squares, tucking the

corners under the sides of the green squares. Tack in place.

10 Finally, fold the edges of the backing fabric to make a square slightly smaller than the front of the quilt, and join the two together by hemming at the back. Make holding stitches through all layers at the centers of the sides of the inner and outer flowers, and the outside points of the leaves. These will hold the batting in place, as well as the flowers and leaves. Remove all the tacking.

cheater's cushion

This project is for people who like doing the folding but find it boring to make the cushion! Cushions with silk covers in a plain color can be bought in most large department stores in all shapes and sizes, and I have added an appliqué panel of origami-style folded silk squares to the front of this one to make an unusual decorative feature.

For the appliqué I used a piece of silk that was woven in such a way that each side was a different color, but two pieces of silk in different colors, bonded together back to back, would work just as well. Use fusible webbing to bond the squares before you start.

Project by Wendy Lowes   *Size: 16½ x 16½in (41.5 x 41.5cm) cushion, 10½ x 10½in (26.5 x 26.5cm) appliqué panel*

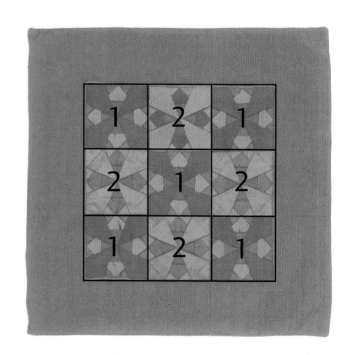

MATERIALS:

❖ One ready-made 16½in (41.5cm) cushion with a removable silk cover in a plain color
❖ Nine 7½in (18.5cm) squares of double-sided medium blue/dark blue silk

OR

❖ Nine 7½in (18.5cm) squares of plain silk in dark blue
❖ Nine 7½in (18.5cm) squares of plain silk in medium blue
❖ 2yds (180cm) of 12in (30cm) wide fusible webbing, cut into 9 squares, 7½in (18.5cm) each
❖ Matching thread to stitch down
❖ 7in (18cm) square of lightweight cardboard

COLOR LAYOUT

The appliqué panel is 10½in (26.5cm) square. Arrange the individual blocks alternately light, dark, light to make a checkerboard pattern.

instructions ▶

1 If you need to bond two pieces of silk to get your double-sided square, follow the instructions on page 22.

2 Fold the edges of a silk square over the cardboard template, as shown on page 64. Fold five with the dark side turned back and four with the light side turned back.

3 At the center of each side, cut two snips 1½in (4cm) apart, to the fold line only. Fold the edge between the two snips over to the reverse side.

4 Starting with the main folded edges facing down, fold the square to Wendy's Base. (See page 24.)

5 Fold as for the leaves on page 55, steps 3–7.

6 Fold the inner points (with the exposed turned-over edges) back to the outside edge of the square.

7 If you have made the cushion cover and still have some of the fabric, or if you have some other silk fabric in the same color as your cushion cover, place a 3in (7.5cm) square of that fabric inside the folded square, tucking edges under.

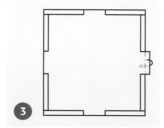

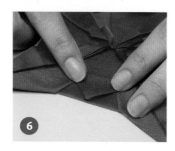

8 Fold the petals down to the center of the square.

9 If you do not have any silk fabric in the same color as your cushion cover, you can cheat!

After step 6, turn the folded square over and mark a 2¾in (7cm) long diagonal cross in the middle of the back. With sharp scissors, carefully cut the cross and fold the four triangles of fabric back. The points will extend beyond the edge of the square, but you can fold them under.

10 Turn the square over to the right side; fold the petals down to the center, and you will see spaces that will show the background fabric when the appliqué block is stitched down in place.

A thin piping strip or cord in matching color around the edge of the appliqué panel gives a professional finishing touch.

11 Repeat the sequence on all nine squares, folding five with the darker color on the outside, and four with the lighter color on the outside.

12 Join the blocks together in three rows of three, with ladder stitch or overcast stitch at the back, following the color layout on page 58. As you sew, catch down the folded points at the center of each side of every block.

13 Center the panel on one side of your cushion cover and pin or tack into place. You will need to put a magazine or a sheet of acetate or card inside the cushion cover, so that you do not stitch right through to the other side!

14 Sink small back stitches along the join-lines between the blocks. Join the points of the petals together with a cross stitch in the center of each square. Hem neatly all round the edge of the panel, catching down the folded points at the centers of the outside edges of the blocks.

op art twist

For several years, I was trying to do this twist fold in fabric by following the instructions in Origami books—it involved a lot of very intricate pre-creasing which is necessary if you are doing it in paper. Then, in 1996, I attended a workshop run by Linda Kemshall, in which she taught this very simple pinch-and-pin method of getting the same effect. She told me that she got the idea from an article by Julie Richardson in the *Quilter* magazine in the summer of 1986, and she called it the JR Square. Both Julie and Linda had their own interesting variations added to the basic twist and I am going to show you my variation inspired by the top of one of Tomoko Fuse's origami boxes. It is wonderful how new ideas get sparked off from one person to another down the years.

If this is folded in plain fabric, it makes an interesting pattern of folds and shadows. Done in a striped fabric, as shown here, you get a wonderful 'op-art' effect and the pattern will vary with stripes of a different width.

Project by Wendy Lowes   *Size: 18 x 18in (45 x 45cm)*

MATERIALS:

FRONT:
- ❖ 1¼yds (113cm) of 42in (105cm) wide striped fabric, cut into 25 squares, 8in (20cm) each
- ❖ Matching thread to sew the squares together
- ❖ 7in (17.5cm) square of lightweight cardboard

BACK:
- ❖ 1¼yds (113cm) of the same fabric as the front, or a plain color to match one of the stripes

INSIDE:
- ❖ 18in (45cm) square pillow form

COLOR LAYOUT

Join the blocks in rows of five, with the direction of the background stripes running alternately horizontally and vertically, both across and down the rows.

instructions ▶

1 Place the cardboard square in the center of the back of your fabric square and iron all the edges over it. This will ensure that the resulting pieces of fabric with their turned-under edges are still perfect squares.

2 Take one square of fabric and make a pinch mark in the center of each side. If a finger pinch does not show enough, use an iron but only press about ⅜in (1cm) at the center of each edge.

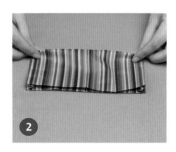

3 Take one pinch with the finger and thumb and move it up to the top edge of that side.

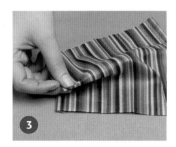

4 Hold all the layers together with a pin in the corner, placed parallel to that side.

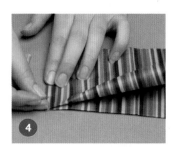

5 Turn once, counter-clockwise, and pick up the pinch on the next side.
  Move the fabric up to the corner on that side and pin again. Repeat on the remaining two sides, turning counter-clockwise each time. There will now be a little balloon of fabric standing up in the middle of the square.

6 Pat this down gently with your hand and it will form a neat diamond

shape folded in the center of the square.

7 Press the central shape flat with an iron.

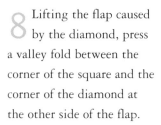

8 Lifting the flap caused by the diamond, press a valley fold between the corner of the square and the corner of the diamond at the other side of the flap.

9 The origami diagram shows the first fold made on the right, with arrows to indicate the next three folds to be made.

10 Repeat this fold on the other three sides.

11 The end of the last triangle will have to be tucked under the first to make the pattern even.

12 To keep the folds in place, sew a few holding stitches at the eight junctions of the folds in the center of the square.

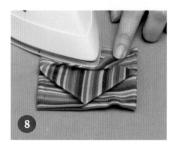

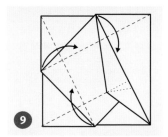

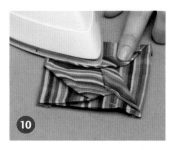

13 Join the folded blocks together in five rows of five with ladder stitch or small overcast stitches at the back.

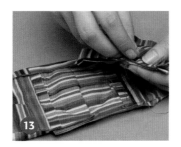

14 For maximum op-art effect, alternate the direction of the stripes on adjacent blocks.

15 To make the back of the cushion cover, cut two pieces of fabric, 20 x 12in (47.5 x 30cm). Make a small hem on one long side on both pieces. Overlap the two hemmed sides to create a 20in (47.5cm) square; pin together; then sew a line of stitching close to the outside edge on both sides to hold the overlap in place.

16 Place the right side of the folded blocks onto the right side of the back and sew the outside edges together along the seam lines. Zigzag the raw edges to prevent fraying.

Turn the cushion cover to the right side through the opening across the back, and use the same opening to insert the pillow form.

TIP

- If the stripes on your fabric have an irregular design of thicknesses and colors, try to position the template in the same place on the pattern each time.
- If the fabric has wider stripes, you could make the cushion with larger squares.
- For other sizes, you always need to start with a square of fabric twice the width and twice the length of the finished block.
- If you think that the opening at the back is too loose, you can add a few snaps or Velcro spots to keep it closed.
- For instructions on inserting a zipper into the back of a cushion, see page 97.

The folds make the stripes in the fabric change direction, creating a fantastic op-art effect.

windsurfers

Looking at a partial drawing of a piece of Cathedral Window patchwork, the shape reminded me of a windsurfing sail with its curved handle across the middle. This inspired me to experiment to see if I could get the effect of sails and water in folded fabric. Firstly, I folded the shape in a square of tissue paper and colored in the sail and the water with crayons. Then I unfolded the square again and looked to see where the patches of color were positioned on the paper. To do the same thing on fabric, I used fabric transfer paint.

I made this wall hanging using folded squares of five different sizes and printing the design in several different colors, which gives the effect of a flotilla of windsurfers sailing across the surface of a lake into the far distance.

Project by Wendy Lowes   *Size: 15 x 28½in (38.5 x 71.5cm)*

MATERIALS:

❖ 1⅛yds (101.25) of good quality, non-shiny, white polyester or other synthetic fabric to cut:
   One 12in (30cm) square
   Seven 8in (20cm) squares
   Eleven 6in (15cm) squares
   Seven 4in (10cm) squares
   Five 3in (8cm) squares
   These sizes include hems
❖ Good quality typing paper on which to paint:
   One 12in (30cm) square
   Two 8in (20cm) squares
   Three 6in (15cm) squares
   Two 4in (10cm) squares
   Two 3in (8cm) squares

The second set of numbers is different because you can get up to four decent prints from one painting
❖ Some white tissue paper and colored pencils to design your sails
❖ Fabric transfer paints: Blue and green for the water, brown for the masts and a selection of colors for the sails
❖ Matching threads for stitching down different parts of the squares
❖ Blue-green size 5 pearl cotton to join the squares

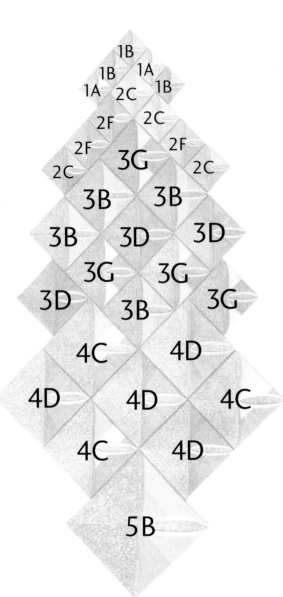

COLOR LAYOUT

1A is a 3in (8cm) block with blue and white sails

1B is a 3in (8cm) block with orange and yellow sails

2C is a 4in (10cm) block with green and yellow sails

2F is a 4in (10cm) block with blue and red sails

3B is a 6in (15cm) block with yellow and orange stripe sails

3D is a 6in (15cm) block with blue and red diamond sails

3G is a 6in (15cm) block with blue and white diamond sails

4C is an 8in (20cm) block with green, white, and yellow stripe sails

4D is an 8in (20cm) block with blue and red diamond sails

5B is a 12in (30cm) block with yellow and orange stripe sails

instructions ▶

1 Fold a 12in (30cm) square of white tissue paper, as for Cathedral Window (see page 15).

After the corners have been folded in twice, roll back the edges only on one side of the diagonal (see diagram).

Using a blue pencil, color the left side and the shape showing through the rolled-back edges. Color the half rolled-back diagonal brown for the mast. The two triangles top and bottom right will be the sail.

Unfold the whole piece to see where the blocks of color are positioned.

Repeat the above for the other four size squares, referring to the color layout and using different designs and colors for the sails.

2 Using the fabric transfer paint on squares of typing paper, paint a mirror image of what you see on the tissue paper. Allow the paint to dry.

3 Place the painted side of the paper down onto the matching size square of fabric. Tape in position with masking tape around the edges, to prevent it from moving. Iron the back of the paper until the image is transferred to the fabric. To test, you can lift one corner to see how it looks.

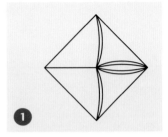

TIP

- Remember that the initial painting is a mirror image of the finished print.

- The base fabric has to be synthetic to give a vibrant and lasting color.

- The transfer paint will look much darker on the typing paper than the color will print onto the fabric.

- You can transfer up to four times with each painting.

4 When you have finished all the printing, you can start folding, using an iron. With the printed side down, fold in all the side edges.

5 Find the center of the square by putting the diagonally opposite corners together and making a pinch mark in the middle. Do the same with the other diagonal —where the two pinch marks cross is the center.

6 With the print-side down, fold the corners to the center of the square. The most accurate way of doing this is illustrated on page 24.

7 Slip-stitch the edges together.

8 This is how it looks on the other side.

9 With the slip-stitched side facing up, fold the corners to the center and hold them in place with a cross stitch.

10 On the sail side, roll back the folded edges and stitch down, as for Cathedral Window patchwork (see page 15).

11 On the water side, slip-stitch the edges together and hem down the center line.

12 Complete all the different size squares in the same way.

13 Position the blocks as shown in the diagram on page 68, and tack onto firm brown paper, leaving a tiny but equal gap between each square. Using the blue-green pearl cotton, stitch between the squares with twisted insertion stitches, also called faggoting. The insertion stitches will allow a slight movement of the hanging when it is hung on a pin, about one inch away from the wall. When all the stitching is complete, remove the tacking and brown paper.

This detail shows the different types of stitching used in this project.

twist & shout

Twist and Shout is a traditional pinwheel wallhanging. I made my first pinwheel quilt in 1988, but it wasn't until I joined the British Origami Society that I realised how many other pinwheels there are; this is the simplest. When laid together in regular square settings, the holes between units are larger than in the twisted version (see page 74). The backs of these units are flat squares with four triangles projecting out behind; each triangle reaches along half the side of the square. This technique is great for using up odd pieces of fabrics.

The finished piece has been made as a room divider or window blind, but you can just keep adding units until it's the size you want. The step-by-step photos use small pinwheels that start off as 2¾in (7cm) squares, while the wallhanging uses 6½in (16.5cm) squares. The construction principle is the same whatever the size.

Project by Louise Mabbs   *Size: 44 x 44in (110 x 110cm)*

MATERIALS

❖ ¾yd (45cm) each of 42in (105cm) wide cotton fabric in the colors listed. From each fabric, cut 17 squares, each 6½in (16.5cm).
   Maroon (M)
   Red (R)
   Orange (O)
   Yellow (Y)
   Green (G)
   Turquoise (T)
   Royal blue (B)
   Purple (P)
   Violet (V)
❖ ⅜yd (22.5cm) of 42in (105cm) wide cotton fabric in black (X), cut into nine squares, each 6½in (16.5cm)
❖ 9 transparent rings for hanging

COLOR LAYOUT

Pair up the colored squares, right sides together. Make nine pairs with maroon outside and one of each of the other colors inside. Use black inside the last unit instead of maroon on both sides. Repeat with the other colors. The letters on the chart show the outside/inside color of each unit.

MX	RM	OM	YM	GM	TM	BM	PM	VM
MR	RX	OR	YR	GR	TR	BR	PR	VR
MO	RO	OX	YO	GO	TO	BO	PO	VO
MY	RY	OY	YX	GY	TY	BY	PY	VY
MG	RG	OG	YG	GX	TG	BG	PG	VG
MT	RT	OT	YT	GT	TX	BT	PT	VT
MB	RB	OB	YB	GB	TB	BX	PB	VB
MP	RP	OP	YP	GP	TP	BP	PX	VP
MV	RV	OV	YV	GV	TV	BV	PV	VX

instructions ▸

1 First make bagged squares; chain piece the pairs of squares together, right sides together if using patterned fabric, with a short machine stitch and ¼in (6mm) seam allowance. Start two-thirds down one edge, sew around three full sides and on the last side leave a gap of about 1in (2.5mm) between the first and the last stitch.

2 Cut off each corner at more than a 90° angle, so they will not overlap inside when the units are turned inside out.

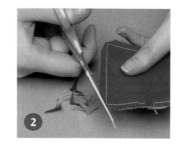

3 Turn the units inside out. Use a blunt knitting needle to gently push the corners out, being careful not to push through the seam. Roll the seam edges between your fingers and finger crease before pressing with a steam iron—this will avoid creases forming and distortion along the edges.

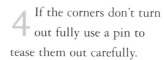

4 If the corners don't turn out fully use a pin to tease them out carefully.

5 Thread a short thin needle with the same thread that the unit was stitched in. Bring it up through the opening on the fold about ¼in (6mm) away.

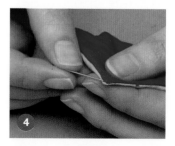

6 Close the hole with ladder stitch, using stitches as small as possible. Begin and end with a tiny overcast stitch so the thread doesn't pull out.

7 Finger press the unit in half to make a rectangle shape. Start in the middle and run your thumbs out toward the edges, using your nails to press the fold into the fabric. On larger units, you can use an iron instead. Turn the unit round by 90° and fold across at right angles to the original fold line.

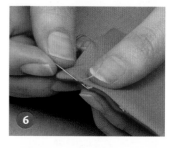

8 Using thread the same color as the inside of the unit, knot the free end then run the needle along the seam a short way and oversew to secure the end of the thread, bringing the point up at the end of a crease line.

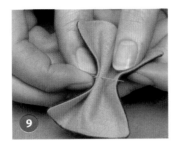

9 Pick up a couple of threads of the fabric where the two creases cross and then pick up a few threads on the opposite edge.

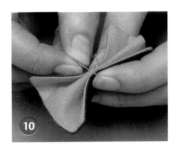

10 Pull the edges together and take two overcast stitches through all layers.

11 Repeat steps 8 and 9 on the remaining two sides, passing the needle under the first stitches in step 9, and pulling the sides into the center. Overcast as before then fasten off the thread down one of the seams.

12 Finger crease the diagonal folds of the unit. On larger units you can iron the creases after finger pressing them.

13 Push two opposite halves of the unit flat, turn over and crease the edges of the square, between the two diagonal folds you have just made. Fold the unit in the opposite direction and finger crease the other two sides of the back square.

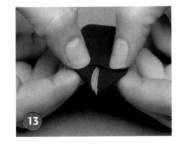

14 Press the units flat with the points folded out to form a pinwheel. To construct the hanging, start by sewing all the vertical columns first. With pinwheels flat, sew the lower right diagonal seam to the upper left of the next unit.

15 Sew the units from the reverse, with a small ladder stitch.

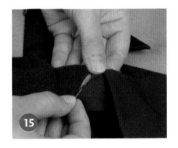

16 Sew column 1 to column 2 pulling the points down to meet on the diagonal folds.

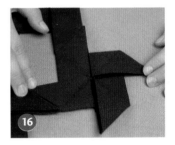

17 Bring your needle up on a corner of the outer row of squares behind the triangle flaps, make a loop and pull the needle through to secure the end, or overcast with tiny stitches.

18 Tack down all the loose flaps around the edges of the hanging and on the back, or the hanging will twist and sag. There is no need to quilt these units but you could add beads on joins and points.

19 Use an overcast stitch to sew rings onto the squares on the back of the top row of units, making sure they lie in the center of the triangle points. Thread a small rod through the rings.

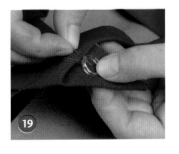

black & white & red all over

When I made my 'Origami Winds'—as in 'the wind blows'—for a quilt exhibition in 1988 in a converted windmill, I wanted to make a piece based on plastic children's wind toys. I remember looking at Robert Harbin's early origami books and seeing the traditional pinwheel, but I didn't like the way the wings only came part of the way along the sides, leaving huge gaps, so I experimented with different fold structures. When I tried to do it again recently I was totally baffled, and it was only when Nick Robinson of the British Origami Society explained Philip Shen's pinwheel to me that I saw how three dimensional the center is—although I have not yet seen a picture or set of instructions which explains this clearly. I hit upon the idea of twisting the center—a technique I've since seen on origami boxes. In paper this is quite hard to do but in fabric it is extremely easy.

In 'Origami Winds' I inserted stuffed square pockets between the pinwheels, which held the structure together, but in this new project I was brave enough to leave the holes. However, on my first attempt, when I held part of the hanging up all the pinwheels unfolded under the weight, so I had to adapt my method!

Project by Louise Mabbs   *Size: 48 x 88in (120 x 220cm)*

MATERIALS

❖ 2½yds (225cm) of 42in (105cm) wide white cotton fabric cut into 51 squares, each 8in (20cm)

❖ 2½yds (225cm) of 42in (105cm) wide black fabric cut into 51 squares, each 8in (20cm)

❖ 2½yds (225cm) of 42in (105cm) wide gray cotton fabric cut into 51 squares, each 8in (20cm)

❖ 153 assorted 8in (20cm) squares of geometric patterned fabric, a mixture of stripes, dots and checks in red and white or black and white

❖ 9 white D rings to hang the finished room divider

❖ 9in (22.5cm) of strong white twill tape as wide or wider than the inside of the flat part of the D ring

❖ Black, white and gray thread to match fabrics

COLOR LAYOUT

Pair a plain and a patterned square together. Make up sets of 4 or 8 units the same if you want a symmetrical pattern.

Rounds 1 & 2: white background (red and white centers)

Round 3: mid gray background

Round 4: dark gray background

Round 5: black

Round 6: red and white stripes

Round 7: mid gray or red and white checks

Round 8: red

Round 9: red and white

Round 10: black and white

Round 11: dark gray

Round 12: black

Round 13: red and white (corners)

TIP

- Cotton works best.

- Stripes work particularly well on this fold because the direction changes as the twist is formed.

- You need twice as many squares of fabric as the final number of units you want.

- Once you have established the final size of your pinwheel you can add or subtract units from the width or length to make the size of room divider you need.

- Make sure you consider the balance of the inside colors in the twisted center, and the outside colors, which form the reverse of the divider. You want it to be dramatic on both sides.

- The Trip Around The World layout works well in this setting. Start with a square, add units to each side to form a cross. Add units onto each arm and in between to create a diamond. Continue adding rounds to the diamond until it is as wide as you want it. After that just add V-shape lines to the top and bottom until the hanging is the length you want it to be.

instructions ▸

1 Using a short machine stitch, sew the squares together in pairs of one plain and one patterned, right sides together. Start halfway down one side, pivot on the needle at each corner and continue all around leaving gap of about 1in (2.5cm). Trim the corners at a larger than 90° angle so the seam allowances will not overlap inside when the units are turned inside out.

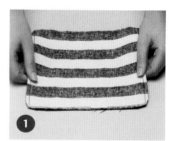

2 Turn the unit inside out and gently push out corners with a blunt knitting needle, then use a pin to gently pull out the corners from the outside (see page 72). Fold the unit back and forth on itself into thirds.

3 Mark the edge of each fold at both ends with a pin.

4 Unfold, then fold the unit diagonally, matching the corners at each end, and take the pin through the other layer.

5 Bring a needle up along the inside fabric of the seam to the pin, remove the pin and overcast through both layers of fabric three times to hold the layers together at this point.

6 Bury the thread in the fold then snip the thread. Repeat on the opposite side.

7 Fold the unit so the stitched joins meet in the center, pin the remaining two corners and then stitch as in step 5.

8 When all four corners are sewn, take hold of two of them.

9 Twist the corners in a counterclockwise direction.

10 You should have four interlocking triangles in the center, with four right-angle triangles on the edges. All the sewn joins should lie on top of the corners of the four outer triangles.

11 Check to make sure the square that has been created on the reverse of the unit by this twist fold is straight, and adjust as necessary.

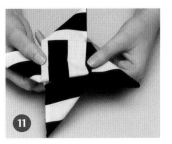

12 Press the folds from the reverse. Lift the flaps so you can press each outer triangle fully.

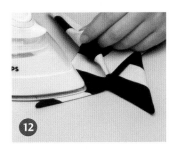

13 Flatten the unit and press the square on the reverse side, then turn the unit over and iron all the interlocking triangles from the front.

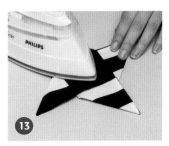

JOINING THE UNITS

14 Lay out your units to create the design you want, using small safety pins to hold them in order until you are happy with the layout. Alternatively you can pin them to a pinboard. Start by joining two diagonal edges of the pinwheel together. Lay them right sides together, bring your needle up through the fold of the corner facing you. Use a single knot and pop it through into the fold then do a little overcast stitch right on the corner to stop the thread from pulling through.

15 Take the needle through the outside edge of the back unit where the corner was joined and then through the corner of the square behind it. Pull up the three folds together and join them with an overcast.

16 Continue sewing the diagonal folds together with a small ladder stitch. At the other end of the seam, pick up the outside triangle at the join again, plus the corner of the square. Pull all three folds together, overcast a couple of times, then bury the end of the thread along one of the folds. The two units are now joined at the back (as shown here).

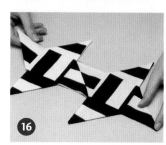

17 This picture shows the front of the unit. Stitch any loose triangles down around the edge of the hanging, since they are not caught onto other units and will gape open. Quilting is not necessary, but you can add a bead, or tie the center of the crossover triangles.

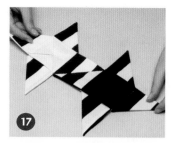

FINISHING

18 Sew rings onto the back of the squares along the top row of the hanging. Since the pinwheels may distort under their own weight, use D rings fixed with lengths of wide tape. Cut a piece of tape about 1in (2.5cm) long. If it is wider than the inside flat part of the D ring, fold in the edges so it is the same width. Appliqué the tape behind the square.

19 Lay the D ring on top of the tape and roll the raw edge of the tape over it, so you can't see it from the front of the square. Hold the triangle flaps out of the way while you stab stitch the tape round the ring, through all layers of the square. Use thread to match the pinwheel or place stitches in strategic places so they are invisible.

20 Turn the remaining raw edges of the tape under and overcast down.

The reverse side of the hanging can be just as dramatic as the front, particularly when the stripes change direction.

present adventures

I used to have a studio/shop in Derbyshire and one Christmas I made an Advent quilt for the window display. When I got married we each used to hang twelve small presents off large beads on the quilt and we took turns opening one on alternate days. When the children came along we included them, girls one day, boys the next. As the presents come off, decorations go on. The quilt now hangs by our front door and visitors are given gifts too—although these days my quilting group buys my presents as my husband gave up!

This project is a rather more sophisticated version and will hold larger presents. I have great fun finding little presents for everyone, hunting in charity shops and sales throughout the year to fill all the pockets, hence the title.

Project by Louise Mabbs *Size: 41 x 51in (102.5 x 127.5cm)*

MATERIALS

❖ 25 pieces of 5½ x 7½in (14 x 18.5cm) metallic
   fabric for the background blocks, in the following colors:
   5 silver
   5 gold
   5 red
   5 green
   5 blue
❖ 25 pieces of 3 x 4in (7.5 x 10cm) metallic fabric
   for the numbers, in the following colors:
   12 silver
   13 gold
❖ ⅞yd (79cm) of 12in (30cm) wide fusible webbing, cut
   into 25 pieces, 3 x 4in (7.5 x 10cm) each
❖ ⅞yd (79cm) of 42in (105cm) wide red cotton fabric, cut
   into 25 pieces, 5½ x 7½ins (14 x 18.5cm) each
❖ ⅞yd (79cm) of 42in (105cm) wide green cotton fabric,
   cut into 25 pieces, 5½ x 7½ins (14 x 18.5cm) each

❖ 1¼yds (113cm) of 42in (105cm) wide blue cotton fabric,
   cut as follows:
   4 strips, 3in (7.5cm) x the fabric width for the vertical
   the sashing
   20 pieces 3 x 5½in (7.5 x 14cm) for horizontal sashing
   4 strips, 3½in (9cm) x the fabric width for the borders
   Depending on the width of your fabric, you may find it
   necessary to cut an extra strip to add length to the borders
   and vertical sashing.
❖ 1½yds (135cm) of 42in (105cm) wide cotton fabric for
   the backing
❖ 1 piece of 45 x 52in (113 x 130cm) lightweight batting
❖ Red and blue thread to join pockets and blocks
❖ Gold lurex thread to appliqué numbers
❖ Gold lurex hand quilting thread or blue or red machine
   quilting thread
❖ 100 star sequins in 5 different shapes (optional)
❖ Decorative buttons to hold flaps down (optional)

COLOR LAYOUT

Lay out the background block metallic fabrics in a five x five grid, with the colors balanced. Lay the blue sashing strips between them and pin all the pieces to a pinboard or sheet so you can sew the blocks in the right order. Pair up pieces of red and green fabric for the pockets and decide which will be the front color and which the back, balancing them in relation to one another and the background blocks. The diagram above shows the quilting order. Start at 1 and stitch to the end of the arrow—dotted lines indicate where you run the needle between the layers of fabric to reach the next block. Repeat with line 2 and so on until line 18.

> ### TIP
> - *Before starting to quilt, first tack or safety pin the layers together, to hold them in position as you work.*
> - *The quilting diagram above is for lap quilting, which is easier to work from the corners inwards. If you are quilting on a frame, work from the center diagonal, out to the corners.*
> - *I find it helpful to weight the center of the quilt on a table with heavy books and then tension the corner I am sewing, with my body against the table edge, so both hands are free to stitch.*

instructions ▶

BASIC QUILT

1 Pin the metallic blocks and horizontal sashing together, placing the pins in the seam allowance to avoid marking the metallic fabric. Stitch together with ¼in (6mm) seams, then iron the seams towards the sashing. Pin the columns to the vertical sashing, then add the side, top and bottom borders.

NUMBERS

2 Iron fusible webbing onto the back of the silver and gold metallic fabric for the numbers, leaving the backing paper in place. Draw up the numbers 1–25 to the size you want on thin paper. Cut around each number with a small margin and center them on the right side of the metallic fabric. Cut through paper template and fabric together.

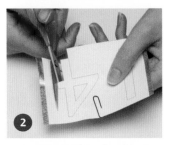

3 For inside holes, fold the number along a straight line, cut a small slot across the fold to slip the scissors into, then cut as normal.

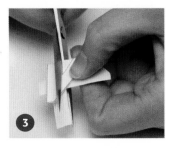

4 Use the negative cut-out of the number to space double numbers on the right sides of the pocket fabric. Remember that Advent calendars usually have numbers scattered at random, so that you have to hunt for the correct number each day.

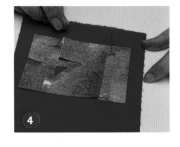

> ### TIP
> - *Try using a computer to print out outline numbers to the correct size to use as a template.*
> - *If the pieces slip when you cut the numbers, use paper clips to hold the paper and fabric together, as pins will mark the metallic fabric.*

5 Pull off the fusible webbing backing paper on the numbers then replace them in the negative cut-out for position. Iron in place on the pocket fabric pieces.

6 Set your machine stitch to a medium zigzag, with metallic thread on top and plain cotton beneath. Stitch around the numbers, leaving enough thread to pull the ends through to the back and knot, so they don't unravel. Iron carefully, protecting the metallic fabric.

POCKETS

7 Take each piece of pocket fabric with a number and pair up with the other color—red with green and vice versa. With right sides together, starting on the edge below the number, stitch all around leaving a gap of 1in (2.5cm) halfway along the bottom edge.

8 Trim off the corners and turn the pockets inside out. Roll the edges with your fingers then iron carefully, especially over the numbers. Ladder stitch the gap closed.

9 Place the pockets on the quilt and stitch each in place with red thread close to the edge, turning back top corners at random to add interest to the layout. Backstitch at the start and

end, pull the thread ends through to the back and knot firmly. The weight of the gifts may pull the pocket, so this will make it stronger.

QUILTING

10 Stretch and pin the quilt as described on page 127. Hand quilt around each pocket just beyond the seam allowance—see the plan on page 82. Use metallic thread and a fairly long stitch. A long needle will enable you to sew several stitches in one go. Quilt ⅝in (17mm) in from the edge around the border. Add a sequin to the thread at the corner of each block.

FINISHING

11 To self-bind the edges, trim the batting and backing level with the edge of the border and fold the border fabric to the quilting line. Fold the backing and batting raw edges in.

12 At each corner, fold the fabric under in a straight fold with no miter.

13 Stitch the top border down to the back border with an invisible appliqué stitch. Add the tube for the hanging rod across the top of the back of the wall hanging, as described on page 127.

> **TIP**
> - Using a needle with a larger eye helps to prevent the metallic thread from breaking, but if the needle is too large it will leave huge holes in the metallic fabric.
> - When ironing the metallic fabric, use Teflon or baking parchment and a medium heat to protect it.

> **TIP**
> - When hand sewing with metallic thread, move the thread along a little after each couple of stitches, so the eye of the needle does not wear the outer core of the thread away.

pineapple, mango, papaya

I originally trained as a weaver and knitter, so I'm always thinking of ways to combine these skills with my quiltmaking. This project is based around weaving folded strips of fabric, is quick to do and is a good technique for using up scraps of fabric left over from other projects. Each place mat is square and the runner is simply three mats joined together with sashing strips. The instructions are for mats with even weaving, but you can have great fun playing around with different weaves, strip widths, and color arrangements, as shown here in the end square of the runner. If you added batting you could make a bed quilt using the same technique.

Project by Louise Mabbs *Size: 11 x 11in (27.5 x 27.5cm) mat, 11 x 35in (27.5 x 87.5cm) runner*

MATERIALS

FOR EACH MAT:

❖ ⅝yd (56.5cm) of 42in (105cm) wide cotton fabric in each of the colors listed. Cut each piece into 20 strips 3 x 11in (7.5 x 27.5cm)
Yellow
Orange
Green
Dark blue
Turquoise

❖ ⅛yd (12cm) of 42in (105cm) wide turquoise cotton fabric, cut into 2in (5cm) wide strips across the width on the straight of grain and joined into one single, long length

FOR THE RUNNER:

❖ 1⅞yds (169cm) of 42in (105cm) wide cotton fabric in each of the colors listed. Cut each piece into 60 strips 3 x 11in (7.5 x 27.5cm)
Yellow
Orange
Green
Dark blue
Turquoise

❖ ½yd (45cm) of 42in (105cm) wide turquoise cotton fabric, cut into the following:
Three 2in (5cm) wide strips across the width on the straight of grain, then joined into one long length
Four strips 1½ x 11in (4 x 27.5cm)

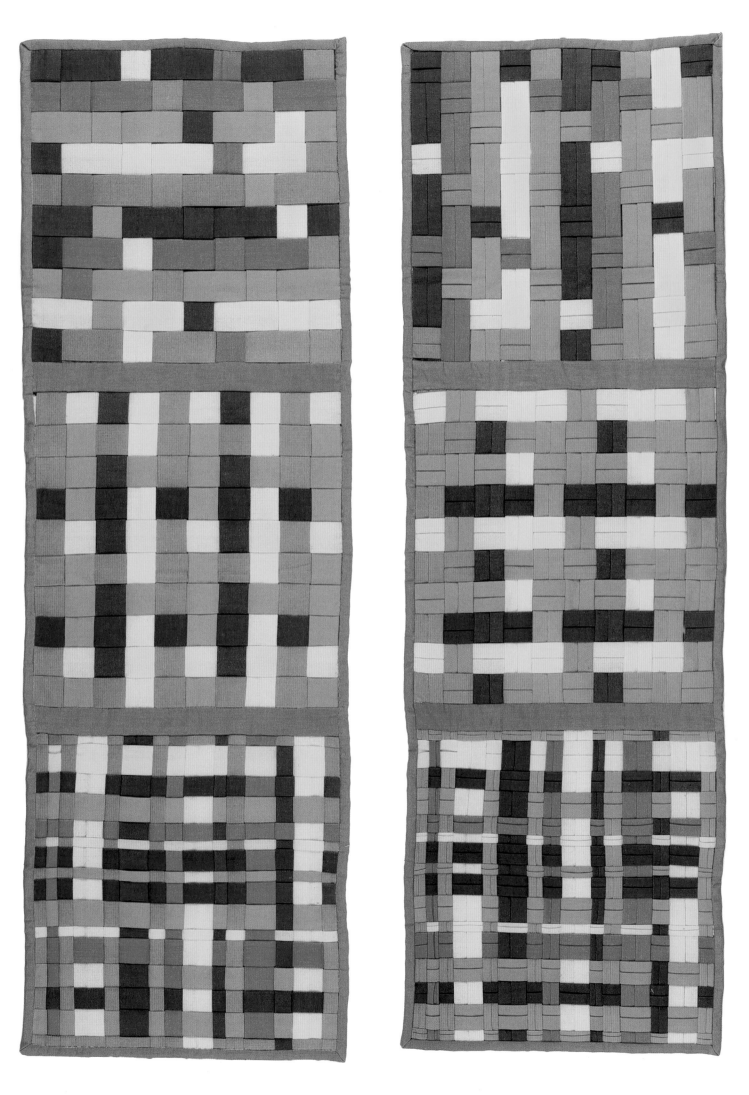

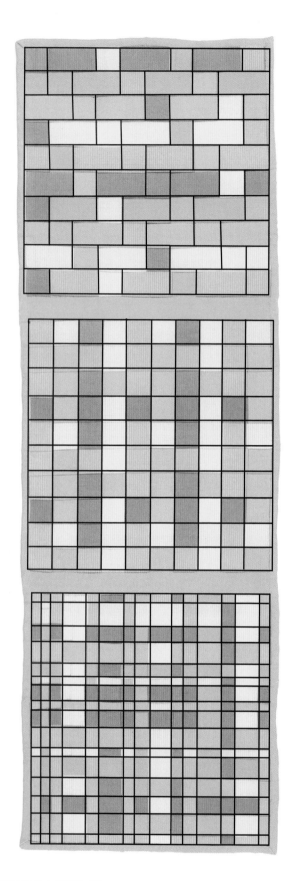

COLOR LAYOUT

Random - with any number of colors.

Planned - use an even number of colors and consider how they will balance in each direction. The diagram above shows the weaving plan for each section of the runner.

TIP

- *If you want to use slippery fabrics, press a strip of fusible webbing under the fold.*
- *To make a bed quilt, use strips 6 x 12½in (15 x 31.5cm), with a 3 x 12½in (7.5 x 31.5cm) strip of batting.*
- *When pressing the strips, if you put half a dozen horizontally in front of you and press the nearest first, by the time you have finished at the back the nearest one will be cool enough to manipulate again.*
- *If you go for a more complex weave, such as a twill in which the numbers of overs and unders are varied, you will need to stitch the strips in place as the weave will be less stable.*
- *You can also trap small Prairie or Somerset points between the folds, although you will need to stitch them in place.*

instructions ▶

1 Fold over and press 1in (2.5cm) along each strip length.

2 Fold the remaining edge over the first flap, so that the whole strip is folded into thirds.

3 Tuck the raw edge of the top layer under to meet the previous fold and press it in place.

4 Lay ten strips side by side, with the folded side up, in the order you want them. Stitch along the top edge of the strips using a scant ⅛in (3mm) seam. Stitch the bottom ends together just to hold the

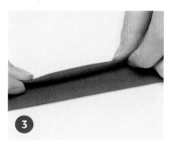

folds in place, but then cut between the strips at the bottom to separate them out again at one end only.

5 Lay the second set of strips side by side in order, with the fold side up, and stitch across both ends as before.

6 Pin the fully-joined set to a pin board or ironing board at the corners to hold it steady as you work. Weave the first, partially-sewn set through the second, pinned down set. Pin the loose ends into the board. Plain weaving is the strongest structure— odd number strips go under/over/under/over, while even number strips go over/under/over/under.

Unpin the block from the board, but pin the loose strips to the block edge. Machine them together and then gently pull the block into shape. Quilting is not necessary, but if you are making a bed quilt with this technique then stitch using a running stitch or machine quilting design along the folded edge, otherwise the unit will gape open.

RUNNER

7 To join three units, use a version of the quilt-as-you-go technique. Lay a joining strip under the block

along one edge and lay another strip on top of the block edge. Stitch in place with a ¼in (6mm) seam, using a short stitch and taking care not to catch the vertical folded strips into the seam—you can push them out of the way and then wriggle the block back into shape after all the edging has been sewn on.

8 Sew the other side of the top strip to the second block. Turn the block upside down, so the back joining strip should then be wrong side up.

9 Fold under ¼in (6mm) on the raw edge of the joining strip to hide the seams. Ladder stitch the folded edge down with short stitches, just beyond the machine stitched line, being carefully to only sew through the top layers of fabric so no stitches show on the front.

TO BIND UNITS

10 Fold and press the binding in half lengthwise with the joining seams pressed open. Start partway along one edge. With the raw edges of the binding along the raw edges of the right side of the block, leave about 2in (5cm) of binding hanging free before you start stitching. Using a short stitch and a ¼in (6mm)

seam sew up to the corner, taking care not to catch the vertical woven strips into the seam. At the corner, lift the presser foot up and move the block away a short distance.

11 Twist the block around ready to sew the second side. Make a fold in the binding so it is level with the previous raw edges —this technique seems to work whatever the width of the binding.

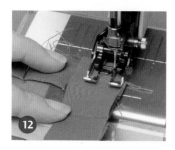

12 Start stitching again, a short way down the raw edge, where the woven strips of the block start again. Continue around the block. Stop stitching 2–3in (5–7.5cm) from the beginning of the binding.

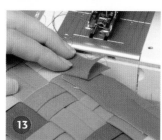

13 Cut the end of the binding off ½in (1.5cm) past the point where you started binding.

14 Open up the binding and stitch a ¼in (6mm) seam. It helps to pin this before you start stitching as it will twist as you sew it.

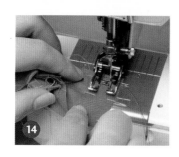

15 Finger press the seam allowance open, then fold the strip in half again. Resume stitching the binding on, between where you started and finished.

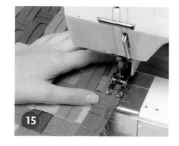

16 Fold the binding over to the wrong side and appliqué it down with a short blind stitch, just beyond the machine stitching line. Be careful just to go through the top layers so no stitches show on the front. When you get to the corner, bring the needle up right on the corner.

17 Fold a miter in the binding at the corner, making sure the fold lies the same direction as it does on the front.

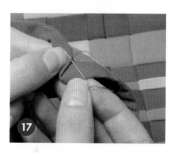

18 Continue blind stitching past the corner miter.

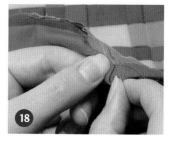

The back of the placemat is smooth, the front has folds. They can look quite different back and front, depending on which weaving pattern you use. As long as you use the same colors for each, they will still look like a matching set.

twist & grout

As a child I remember being rather bored in some church services, so I spent most of the time working out how the old ladies' ornate hats were constructed, or tweed coats were woven, or admiring the beautiful stained glass in the dramatic Norman building. I have loved stained glass windows ever since.

When I was making my first samples for this project, I played around with twisting one end of the flat piping the opposite way to the other. With its black piping, like 'leading' (or grout), between the bright colors, this technique reminds me of the traditional stained glass appliqué technique, but twisting the piping gives it a fantastic three-dimensional quality. The steps show how to make the cushion shown in the main picture opposite, but alternative variations for cushion designs are shown opposite above. These are constructed using exactly the same basic techniques, but the one on the right is batik-style with narrow folded vertical black cotton 'leading', and the one on the left has the color laid in Fibonacci proportions with no vertical bands at all.

Project by Louise Mabbs   *Size: 15 x 15in (37.5 x 37.5cm)*

MATERIALS

❖ 60 pieces of various brightly-colored cotton fabrics each 2½in (6.5cm) long and of varying widths from 1½in (4cm) to 3in (7.5cm) wide, for the 'glass'

❖ ¾yd (68cm) of 42in (105cm) wide black cotton fabric, cut as follows:
  4 strips 1½ x 36in (4 x 90cm) for the twisted 'leading'
  3 strips 1½ x 15½in (4 x 39cm) for the vertical sashing
  2 strips 2½ x 15½in (6.5 x 39cm) for the borders
  2 pieces 10 x 15½in (25 x 39cm) for the back

❖ ½yd (45cm) of 42in (105cm) wide white cotton fabric, cut as follows:
  1 piece 15½in (39cm) square for the front lining
  2 pieces 10 x 15½in (25 x 39cm) for the back lining

❖ 1 piece of batting approximately 15½in x 36½in (39 x 91.5cm), cut as follows:
  1 piece 15½in (39cm) square for the front
  2 pieces 10 x 15½in (25 x 39cm) for the back

❖ 15in (37.5cm) square cushion pad

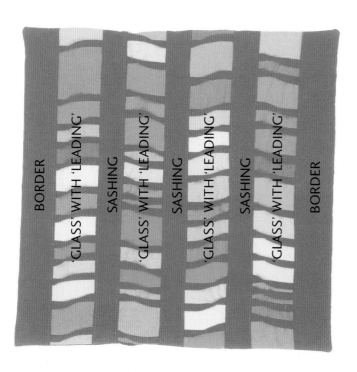

COLOR LAYOUT

The colors in this cushion are laid out randomly, but you can also lay them out in an 'extended rainbow' so they move through the color wheel. The number of colors in the rotation will affect the outcome, so play around with combinations of color and strip width until you are happy.

TIP

- *This is a good project for using up scraps from other projects, although you can also make your units from long fabric strips pieced together into large units and then cut at right angles into shorter strips.*
- *If you lay the colored pieces out in a random pattern rather than the 'extended rainbow' suggested a less repetitive image is achieved, but be careful that the same color doesn't get clumped together in one area.*
- *The finished cushion can have a zipper closure instead of the simple flap opening on the back.*
- *Materials and instructions are given for a rear flap opening, but for instructions on inserting a zipper fastening, see page 97.*

---

instructions ▸

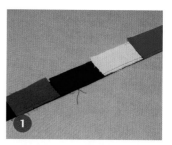

1 Iron the black cotton 'leading' strips in half lengthwise, wrong sides together. Lay the 'leading' out and lay the 'glass' colors on top in your chosen order, with right sides together. Stitch through all three layers of fabric along the raw edge side of the 'leading,' with a seam allowance of less than ³⁄₁₆in (4.5mm).

2 Cut along the edges of the 'glass' pieces with a rotary cutter and lay them out in the same order.

3 Lay the 'glass' of the second unit right sides together against the 'leading' of the first unit and join the first two units together along the original seam, creating a pleat or tuck in the leading. Continue to chain piece the pairs, leaving the last one attached to the machine. Join the pairs into fours and repeat until you have four strips of 'glass' and 'leading' each 15½in (39cm) long.

4 Press the strips from the back with all the seams facing the same direction, then press from the front against the folds to eliminate tucks. Pin one side of the 'leading' the way it is lying naturally, pin the other the opposite way, turning over seam allowances underneath at the same time.

5 Sew down both edges of the strip to hold the ends of the twisted leading in place, stitching ³⁄₁₆in (4.5mm) in from the edge so the stitching will be concealed within the final seam. Sew the 1½in (4cm) strip of black cotton sashing on each side of the strip, leaving a ¼in (6mm) seam allowance.

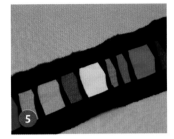

6 Add further strips on each side of this then add the 2½in (6.5cm) strip of black cotton border on each outer edge.

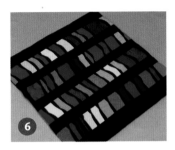

QUILTING

7 Layer the lining fabric, batting and top; pin every 3in (7.5cm) with small safety pins. Machine quilt in the ditch, with a walking/ even pressure/quilting foot, right to the seam allowance. Work slowly to follow the line, especially at seams.

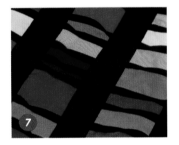

8 For the back, layer the white lining, batting, and black backing, right sides out, and pin every 3in (7.5cm) with small safety pins. Trim the wadding back by ¼in (6mm) along one long edge, fold the black backing over to the white side and hem in place. Using a blunt needle and a ruler, score a series of lines parallel to the hemmed edge, then machine quilt them.

9 For the flap opening, lay one of the back panels on top of the front panel, right sides together with raw edges matching (so about one third of the front still shows). Pin and stitch together with a seam less than ⅛in (3mm). Pin the second back piece on, raw edges matching front, so the two pieces of the back overlap in the middle. Stitch all around the cushion with a ¼in (6mm) seam. Trim off excess fabric at the corners and zigzag all around with a wide open stitch, then turn inside out and poke out the corners carefully with a blunt knitting needle. Insert the pillow form through the flap.

Detail of one of the alternative cushion designs, with the colors laid out in Fibonacci proportions, and twisted 'leading.'

peapods

I came across this idea while experimenting with folded strip techniques and although my first sample was black and is now on the Nip and Tuck quilt (see page 98) the shape of it reminded me of peapods. If you want to make it look even more realistic you could make mini Suffolk Puffs (yo yos) or sew buttons onto your cushions to represent the peas!

If you want to make a bigger cushion, cut as many strips of green as the finished width of the cushion in inches—for example, 18 for a 18in (45cm) cushion, and one less of the colored strip—for example, 17 for a 18in (45cm) cushion. The panel width is one third of the final cushion width (for example, on the 18in (45cm) cushion it would be 6in (15cm) plus seam allowances).

Project by Louise Mabbs   *Size: 15 x 15in (37.5 x 37.5cm)*

MATERIALS

❖ ¾yd (68cm) of 42in (105cm) wide dark green cotton fabric, cut as follows:
  15 pieces 1½ x 5½in (4 x 14cm) for tucks
  2 pieces 5½ x 15½in (14 x 39cm) for front panel sides
  2 pieces 8½ x 15½in (21.5 x 39cm) for back
  1 piece 2 x 15½in (5 x 39cm) the back zipper flap
❖ 14 pieces 1½ x 5½in (4 x 14cm) in a variety of bright colors for the tucks

❖ 1 square 15½in (39cm) white cotton for front lining
❖ 2 pieces 8½ x 15½in (21.5 x 39cm) white cotton for back lining
❖ 2 pieces 8½ x 15½in (21.5 x 39cm) light weight batting
❖ 14in (35cm) long green zipper
❖ 15in (37.5cm) square pillow form

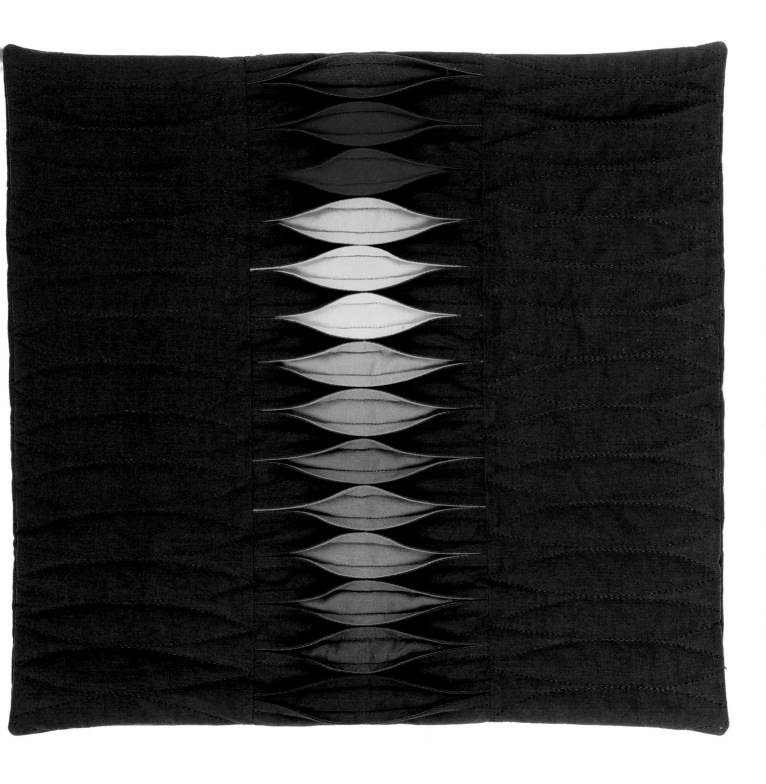

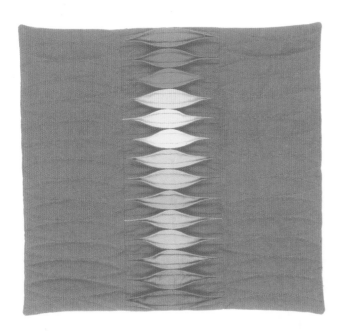

COLOR LAYOUT

Arrange the various colors in an attractive order—I like to arrange them in a spectrum.

TIP

- *The finished cushion can have a flap closure instead of the zipper opening on the back. For instructions on making a flap opening, see page 93.*
- *My technique of inserting the zipper in the cushion back avoids having to oversew the fabric edges together first and also hides the zipper teeth from view and from catching on other furnishings.*
- *If you are hand quilting use safety pins to hold layers together so you don't catch your fingers on the pins.*
- *Using a steam iron helps avoid shiny patches where there is a build up of seam layers.*

instructions ▸

1 Make the front panel by sewing one green strip to the first color strip, then another green strip to the second color strip. Use a scant ³⁄₁₆in (4.5mm) seam allowance. Chain piecing in pairs saves thread and time.

2 When all the pieces are joined, cut all but the last pair off and join the first set of pairs to the second, third to the fourth and so on, until all the strips are joined. Press with all seams going the same direction on the back. If you pull one end of the fabric up and press toward it, the stretch helps eliminate tucks at the joins.

3 Fold the seams along the seam lines and finger press. Stitch the seams with a ¼in (6mm) seam allowance to create a kind of false French seam. Be very careful that your seams remain a constant width, especially at the ends.

4 Press the panel so the colors are hidden and you can only see the green fabric. Pin the tucks closed and stitch them down with a ⅛in (3mm) seam.

5 Pin the two sides to the folded panel, right sides together, and stitch with a ¼in (6mm) seam—it is easier with the panel underneath.

Press on the back with the seams facing outwards. Press any tucks out on the front.

6 Layer the white lining square, batting and front panel, and pin every 3in (7.5cm). Quilt a line down each side of the center panel, just inside the seam lines on the tucks. Quilt peapod shapes (see right) on each side panel, with a medium stitch.

7 On the backing pieces, mark the peapods point to point with those on the front and draw half the design again (the shapes will overhang the edge).

8 To make the back, fold the 2 x 15½in (5 x 39cm) strip lengthwise wrong side together; press. Pin the strip to one long side of the cushion back with the raw edges together and sew with a ⅛in (3mm) seam.

9 Pin the zipper with right side facing the strip, using dressmaker's pins at right angles to the zipper.

10 Stitch close to the teeth with a zipper foot. You will need to move the zipper pull—leave the needle in the zipper and cushion back, lift the presser foot and push the zipper pull up. Once it is out of the way resume stitching. Repeat on

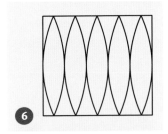

the other side, making sure the two sides of the cushion back are even. Zigzag the edges of the zipper to the raw edges of the back panels.

11 Lay the backing on the front, right sides together and pin. Make sure the zipper flap is lying in the correct direction. Pin and stitch all around with a ¼in (6mm) seam, trim off any excess fabric at the corners and zigzag all around with a wide open stitch. Turn the cover right side out and poke out the corners carefully with a blunt knitting needle.

12 With a dressmaker's chalk pencil and a ruler draw a line down the center of the folded panel. Use a long hand sewing needle and green thread so you can travel the needle between layers to the next catching point. Working along the line, catch the green folded edge of the first tuck with the needle and pull back to reveal the color. Make two tiny overcast stitches to hold the first tuck to the second. Stitch the second tuck to the third tuck until each pair is raised.

13 Between each pair of tucks, take the needle down between the layers and bring it up again midway across the next green strip.

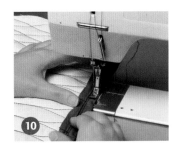

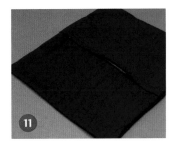

nip & tuck

Many of the blocks in this quilt were my initial samples for this book and I had great fun doing them. I could have gone on forever—there are always far more ideas than time to do them. Technically, piping is a strip of fabric inserted between others, which may be flat or stuffed with a cord. Tucks are stitched folds made in one piece of fabric. Many quilters use the word tuck to describe similar techniques, and in this project 'tuck' is sometimes used to refer to flat piping.

There are at least 17 variations in the way piping is used here and you will probably discover many more. The beauty of a piece like this is that you can build it gradually, making small samples from the off-cuts from different projects, and using a single color, such as black, to unify everything. Just cut up your scraps into strips and stitch them together into a flat fabric, then you can manipulate them once there are enough to do your project—which can be made to any proportion.

Project by Louise Mabbs   *Size: 52 x 65½in (130 x 164cm)*

MATERIALS

❖ 8yds (720cm) of 42in (105cm) wide black cotton fabric, cut as follows:

2 pieces 42 x 60in (105 x 180cm) for the backing

9 strips 1½ x 48½in (4 x 121.5cm) for the sashing

3 strips 1½ x 22in (4 x 55cm) for the sashing

2 pieces of 2 x 58in (5 x 145cm) for borders

2 pieces of 2 x 72in (5 x 180cm) for borders

6 strips of 1 x 42in (2.5 x 105cm) for binding

2 pieces 9 x 42in (22.5 x 105cm) for hanging tube

Use the remaining fabric for the panel backgrounds

❖ Scraps and strips of fabric in a variety of different bright colors. The project illustrated features the following:

Maroon

Dark red

Red

Orange

Salmon

Peach

Yellow brown

Yellow

Lemon yellow

Pale yellow

Yellow green

Light green

Grass green

Bright green

Dark green

Blue green

Dark turquoise

Light turquoise

Light blue

Sky blue

Dark blue

Light purple

Dark purple

Dark fuchsia

❖ 56 x 70in (140 x 175cm) piece of medium weight batting

❖ Black thread

COLOR LAYOUT

The wallhanging is made up of random blocks of black with colored piping and multi-color sequences with black piping. The blocks are assembled with black sashing and backing. Dimensions given are for the finished panels in the quilt, so add another ¼in (6mm) all around for seam allowances when making each block.

Block 1, 27: 2 x 48in (5 x 120cm)

Block 2: 3 x 48in (7.5 x 120cm)

Blocks 3, 4, 5, 6: 4 x 12in (10 x 30cm)

Block 7: 5 x 30in (12.5 x 75cm)

Block 8: 5 x 18in (12.5 x 45cm)

Block 9, 14: 6 x 13½in (15 x 30cm)

Block 13: 6½ x 13½in (16 x 33cm)

Block 10, 12, 15, 17: 10 x 10in (25 x 25cm)

Block 11: 10 x 15½in (25 x 39cm)

Block 16: 6 x 10in (15 x 25cm)

Block 18, 20: 5 x 12in (12.5 x 30cm)

Block 19: 5 x 24in (12.5 x 60cm)

Block 21: 3 x 8½in (7.5 x 21.5cm)

Block 22: 4 x 9in (10 x 22.5cm)

Block 23: 4 x 24in (10 x 60cm)

Block 24: 8½ x 12in (21.5 x 30cm)

Block 25: 3 x 9in (7.5 x 22.5cm)

Block 26: 3 x 24in (7.5 x 60cm)

1 STRAIGHT TUCKS (BLOCKS 1, 19, 20, 25)
See basic techniques on page 20. Use a variety of widths of colored fabrics with black piping between. Stitch all the ends of the tucks in the same direction.

2 TWISTED TUCKS (BLOCKS 2, 4, 5, 16, 27 BOTTOM)
See basic techniques on page 20. Make a panel of irregular width tucks and background strips. Twist all the piping ends on one edge the opposite direction to the direction of construction. Strips can be set into flat borders (Block 4) or fold one

tuck up and the next down so they reflect each other in pairs (Block 27 bottom).

3 FOLDED TUCKS (BLOCKS 3, 8, 18)

See basic techniques on page 20. The folded edge of the tuck is brought up to the seam to create mini wave tucks. The tucks can be sewn flat in between the folds (Block 3) or a small wave created in the middle of a longer tuck (Block 8).

4 ONE END FOLDED TUCKS (BLOCK 27 TOP)

See basic techniques on page 20. On very wide piping, you may have to fold a tuck only halfway because fully twisted tucks would distort the unit too much.

5 ROLLED TUCKS (BLOCK 22)

See basic techniques on page 20. Roll the folded edge of each tuck under so the fold meets the seam underneath— the tuck should project a little way beyond the seam. Stitch all the tucks in the same direction.

6 SQUASHED TUCKS (BLOCK 7)

See basic techniques on page 20. Instead of pressing the tucks in one direction, press each one flat so it is centered over the seam. To create more texture, press the center of

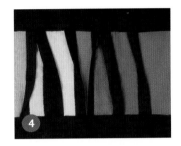

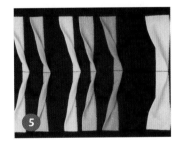

the tucks in one direction creating flattened waves. You can also manipulate the squashed tucks by sewing the edges together by hand or gathering them in with overcast stitches.

7 WAVE TUCKS (BLOCKS 6, 14, 21)

See basic techniques on page 20. Regular width, straight piping manipulated with machine stitching going in opposite directions.

8 CHEVRON TUCKS (BLOCKS 9, 24)

See basic techniques on page 20. Regular width, straight piping is machined in pairs, alternating facing and opposing.

The second line of stitching reverses the pairing. The width of the piping affects whether the chevron tucks cross over one another (Block 9) or butt together (Block 24).

9 FOLDED LOG CABIN (BLOCKS 13 AND PART OF 19)

This is a standard Folded Log Cabin. See basic techniques on page 18.

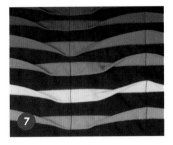

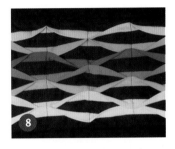

10 RANDOM LOG CABIN TUCKS (BLOCKS 10, 17)

See basic techniques on page 20. Random-shaped black fabric pieces are edged with tucks and joined in irregular layouts. Some tucks are twisted and some of the background pieces are colored rather than black.

11 MULTICOLORED TUCKS (BLOCK 12)

See basic techniques on page 20. The piping is made by sewing alternate strips of black and colored fabrics, then cutting narrow strips off at right angles. Cut a black background vertically, horizontally and diagonally across, and insert tucks into these cuts. See page 107 for more detail of this technique.

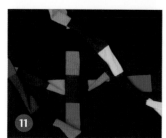

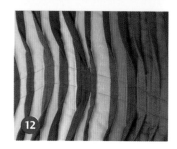

12 BOUND EDGE TUCKS (BLOCK 15 TOP)

See basic techniques on page 20. Stitch random widths together, alternating black and colored strips. Fold the black strips in half, tuck the seam allowances into the black fold and pin seam edges together. Stitch a line parallel to the seams on the colored fabrics. Stitch two parallel lines through the center of the panel in the same direction.

13 MID STRIP TUCKS (BLOCKS 11, 26)

See basic techniques on page 20. Tucks are made in the middle of the fabric piece rather than at the seams, so the tuck is in the same color fabric as its background.

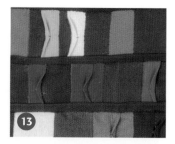

14 SEAM FOLDED TUCKS (BLOCK 15 BOTTOM)

See basic techniques on page 20. Sew regular widths of black and colored fabrics together. Fold and press the strips on the seam lines. Stitch one third in from each edge; the seams will stack up close to each other. Stitch a couple of parallel lines across them to expose varying amounts of color at different parts of the tucks.

15 PEAPODS (BLOCK 23)

See peapod technique on page 96. Sew random width strips, folded on the seams. Stitch a line that contains the previous seam allowances, then catch seams together in pairs on the outside edges, so the colored strips are hidden. Open pairs in the center to reveal the colors and sew the seams together by hand where they meet in the center, or down to the background on wider tucks.

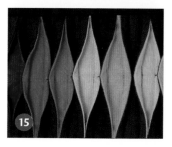

> **TIP**
> - *Using a walking foot helps prevent layers moving.*
> - *Pull thread ends through to the back, knot and lose them in the batting.*

16 HAND-STITCHED TUCKS (BLOCK 11)

See basic techniques on page 20. Pull the edges of a tuck back on itself and catch down with a few small overstitches.

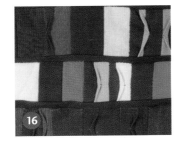

JOINING PANELS

Adjust all the blocks, adding 1½in (4cm) sashing as per the diagram on page 100, until each panel measures the same length. Sew a 1½in (4cm) wide strip of sashing between each panel. Sew a 2in (5cm) wide border on each side and at top and bottom. Machine quilt round the edge of each unit, adding extra lines across long panels.

FINISHING

Trim the batting and backing to the edge of the borders. Stabilize the layers together with a wide and open zigzag stitch. Sew the 1in (2.5cm) binding strips together end to end. Referring to pages 87-88, sew the binding to the quilt and slip stitch in place on the back.

Detail of Block 23, showing the edges of the peapods stitched back to reveal the color beneath.

posies for rosie 2

I made Posies For Rosie I in 2001 as part of an embroidery course. Jean Littlejohn was the instructor and she advised me to use patchwork techniques I already knew but in an unusual way, and fabrics I wouldn't normally use—it even included plastic net vegetable bags! Rosie is my 5-year-old daughter's middle name and she has already made a claim for this new quilt because she's addicted to pink.

I had intended Posies II to be multicolored, but after making some of the samples with the striped fabric I loved the effects so much that I decided to go for a bold look instead. Posies For Rosie I was based on hexagons, whereas here the blocks are simplified by making square bases with snowball or folded square corners. You could simplify this quilt by making all the green triangles the same color and by making the A–F blocks 12½in (31.5cm) square without the white borders, although you may need to start with a block larger than 14in (35cm) square before you manipulate it.

Project by Louise Mabbs *Size: 52½ x 69¼ins (131.5 x 173.5cm)*

MATERIALS

❖ 4½yds (405cm) of 42in (105cm) wide fuchsia cotton fabric, cut as follows:
   12 pieces 14in (35cm) square for blocks A-F
   24 pieces 6½in (16.5cm) square for Blocks 1-9
   2 pieces 36 x 42in (90 x 105cm) for the backing
   1 piece 9 x 52in (22.5 x 135cm) for the hanging tube
   Use the remaining fabric to cut piping
❖ ⅝yd (56.5cm) of 42in (105cm) wide white cotton fabric, cut as follows:
   12 pieces 1 x 11½in (2.5 x 29cm) for Blocks A-F borders
   12 pieces 1 x 12½in (2.5 x 31.5cm) for Blocks A-F borders
   Use the remaining fabric to cut piping
❖ 1⅛yds (101.5cm) of 42in (105cm) wide cotton fabric with 1in (2.5cm) alternate stripes of white and fuchsia for piping

❖ ¼yd (22.5cm) of 42in (105cm) wide dark green cotton fabric, cut into 48 pieces 2½in (6.5cm) square for Blocks 1-9
❖ ¾yd (68cm) of 42in (105cm) wide medium green cotton fabric, cut as follows:
   48 pieces 2½in (6.5cm) square for Blocks 1-9
   3 pieces 12⅞in (32cm) square, cut diagonally into triangles for top and bottom borders
   2 pieces 6⅞in (17cm) square, cut diagonally into triangles for corners
❖ ⅝yd (56.5cm) of 42in (105cm) wide light green cotton fabric, cut as follows:
   3 pieces 12⅞in (32cm) square, cut diagonally into triangles for side borders
   2 pieces 6⅞in (17cm) squares, cut diagonally into triangles for corners
❖ 72 x 52in (180 x 135cm) of medium polyester batting

COLOR LAYOUT

Blocks A–F are fuchsia, with white and fuchsia bias and straight strips insertions and narrow white borders. Blocks 1–9 are log cabin and spiral designs on fuchsia bases with green folded corners. The quilt is squared off with large green triangles.

> ### TIP
> - *If you cannot find fabric in the right colors with a 1in (2.5cm) stripe you can make your own by laying strips of 1in (2.5cm) wide masking tape at 1in (2.5cm) intervals and painting over them with fabric paint.*

instructions ▶

BIAS AND STRAIGHT PIPING

1 For straight piping, just cut strips 2in (5cm) along the grain of the fabric. On the striped fabric cut the strips as you need them, as some blocks use strips cut across the stripes and some feature strips cut along the stripes. For the bias piping, lay your ruler with the 45° angle on the straight edge of your fabric.

2 On large pieces of fabric fold the fabric in half so the cut edge lies on top of itself. Cut into 2in (5cm) strips parallel from the first cut along the bias of the fabric. Keep checking your angle is still accurate—this is easier on large striped fabrics, where you can see if you are veering off line.

3 Straight piping can be joined with regular ¼in (6mm) seams, right sides together. With bias piping, the diagonal ends must face the same way. Lay right sides together. If the stripe runs parallel to the diagonal cut end, match the same color of stripe on the outside edge of each strip. Mark a ¼in (6mm) seam on one edge and pin at right angles, as shown. Check the strips are aligned before trimming the dog-ears at the ends of the seams.

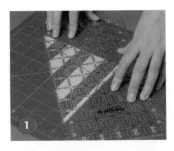

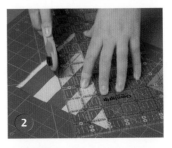

4 If the stripe runs at right angles to the diagonal cut edge, match the stripes across the seam. Mark ¼in (6mm) seam on one edge and pin the edges of the colored stripes on top of each other. Adjust the overhang at each end to ensure proper alignment of the sewn strips. Press the seams open and trim off the dog-ears, then press the piping in half lengthwise.

MAKING BLOCKS A–F

BLOCK A (MAKE 2)

1 This block has a 45° bias cut, straight-line background, with straight white piping. Using a 14in (35cm) fuchsia square, with the wrong side facing up, draw diagonal lines from corner to corner of the background fabric, to form an X.

2 Mark dots every 1–2in (2.5–5cm) along the drawn lines, then cut the background fabric along the marked lines to create four triangles. Stitch a piece of straight white piping onto the bias edge of one of the triangles. Stretch the bias edge as much as you can, while sewing the piping on at normal tension—the end seam will be distorted but will eventually end up flat. Pin a second triangle to this one, matching dots, and

---

> **TIP**
>
> - *The basic principle is to make a block larger than you need, which can then be trimmed down to size, so you start with 35cm (14ins) fuchsia squares.*
> - *Cut along the lines with a rotary cutter. Use a ruler for straight lines, but work freehand for curved.*
> - *Sew the piping on with a seam of just under 4.5mm (³⁄₁₆in). Join seams with a 6mm (¼in) allowance. If possible, use a walking foot for this technique as it will give you more control over the stretch.*

---

stitch. Repeat with the other pair of triangles. Add piping to the bias edge of one of the new triangle sets. Pin the seam together, matching dots, making sure that the first seams are facing in the opposite directions at the intersection. Sew the seam— the bias stretch should relax once the block has been sewn together.

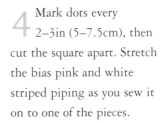

BLOCK B (MAKE 2)

3 This block has a straight cut background with pink and white striped bias piping. Using a 14in (35cm) fuchsia square, with the wrong side facing up, draw three parallel lines at intervals. One of my blocks has the lines spaced 2½in (6.5cm) apart across the center, the other has irregularly-spaced lines.

4 Mark dots every 2–3in (5–7.5cm), then cut the square apart. Stretch the bias pink and white striped piping as you sew it on to one of the pieces.

5 The background should begin to pucker up as the bias relaxes.

6 Pin a second piece to this one, matching dots, and stitch. Stretch the lower layer carefully as you sew the seam. Add the third piece in the same manner.

BLOCK C (MAKE 2)

7 This block has a bias cut curved line background with straight pink and white striped piping. Using a 14in (35cm) fuchsia square, with the wrong side up, draw three freehand curving lines from one edge to the opposite one. Mark dots every 1–2in (2.5–5cm) along the drawn lines, and cut the pieces apart. Stretch the background as you sew the straight pink and white stripe bias on. Pin the seams together at the dots and stretch the top layer as you sew the seam. Everything will ease back to normal after the sewing is complete.

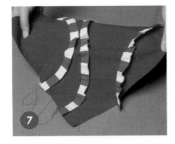

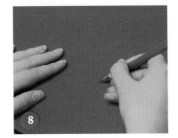

BLOCK D (MAKE 2)

8 This block has inset curves with straight pink and white striped piping. My quilt has a block with a full spiral of bias piping at the bottom, but it is very tricky to make this. Instead you can make two of the alternative Block D, as seen at the top of the quilt. Join the squares so the curve of the piping forms a circle. Using a 14in (35cm) fuchsia square, with the wrong side facing up, cut it into quarters to make four 7in (17.5cm) squares. Draw freehand curves on the wrong side of the fabric from one edge to an adjacent edge, across the corner of the square.

9 Mark dots about every 1–2in (2.5–5cm). When you set the seam together you will need to stretch one side and ease the other—this is where the pencil dots will be essential to match all the pieces up accurately. Hand cut the curves freehand.

10 Stretch the background fabric as much as you can, while sewing the straight pink and white striped piping on at normal tension.

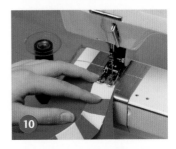

11 Pin the two pieces together, matching all the dots. Stitch with the smaller curve on top, so you can stretch it into the outer curve as you sew.

BLOCK E (MAKE 1)

12 This block has straight of grain cuts with straight pink and white striped piping. Using a 14in (35cm) fuchsia square, use the rotary ruler to draw five lines across, parallel to the edges of your block, and at 2in (5cm) intervals. Mark dots along the lines at 3–4in (7.5–10cm) intervals and cut the pieces apart.

13 Sew a different width piping on each seam—the first two are 1in (2.5cm) wide, the next 1½in (4cm), the fourth 2in (5cm)

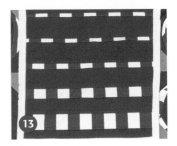

and the last 3in (7.5cm). Pin the seams together, matching the dots.

BLOCK F (MAKE 1)

14 This block has shallow bias cuts with straight pink and white striped piping. Draw three diagonal lines at random across the 14in (35cm) fuchsia square at less than 45° angles. Mark dots every 2–3in (5–7.5cm) and cut the pieces apart.

15 Stretch the background fabric as much as possible as you sew the straight pink and white piping on. Pin the seams together, matching notches and stretch the top fabric as you sew it.

FINISHING BLOCKS A–F

Trim all the blocks down to 11½in (29cm) squares. Add 1 x 11½in (2.5 x 29cm) strips of white cotton to opposite sides. Press the seams outwards. Add 1 x 12½in (2.5 x 31.5cm) strips of white cotton to the other two sides.

MAKING BLOCKS 1–9

1 To prepare the base of the block, fold a 6½ x 6½in (16.5 x 16.5cm) piece of fuchsia cotton in half.

2 Then fold it again, into quarters.

3 Open it out and fold the corners in so the new diagonal fold is the same length as the gap between the corner folds.

BLOCK 1

4 This block has inward spirals in bias pink and white striped piping. Start with the piping on an outside edge of the base with the folded edge of the piping aligned with a diagonal fold line of the octagon, the raw edge toward the center. Ease the strip on as you go—the fold of the piping should be flat and the raw edges slightly puckered; if you don't do this, the strip will stand up too much and raw edges won't be hidden.

5 Continue around to the center, with each subsequent round covering the raw edges of the previous one.

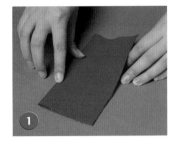

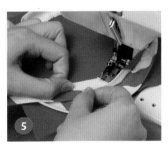

Block 2

6 This block has inward spirals in straight pink and white striped piping. Start with the folded edge of the piping on the outside of the octagon. Make little pleats or gathers as you spiral the piping in towards the center. On the second round, hide the previous round's raw edges.

7 At the center, fold the raw edges of the piping in. Switch to free motion stitching and make a floral motif over the raw edges, or set your machine to a tight zigzag or satin stitch and embroider a spiralling design over the raw edges.

Block 3

8 This block has outward spirals in bias pink and white striped piping. Cut the ends of the bias piping off square and fold in the raw edges at the end of the strip. Lay the tip of the folded strip on the center crease of the base. Curve the strip round so the fold still reaches the center; repeat all the way around to the beginning. On the second round, lay the strip so the previous raw edges are hidden.

TIP
- *Make a variety of spirals and log cabins as below.*
- *The designs can be clockwise or anticlockwise, though clockwise is generally easier to sew.*
- *Vary the fabrics and colors, and even the straight and bias piping in one block, for maximum options.*
- *Use a wide, open zigzag for sewing all these techniques as it stops the edges from fraying. It is decorative, although the edges are mostly not intended to be seen.*

9 Continue to the outer edges until the octagonal area of the base is filled.

Block 4

10 This block has outward spirals in straight pink alternating with white striped piping. Start in the center as in Block 3. By laying the raw edges on flat, corner tucks will appear automatically.

Block 5

11 This block has outward pleated spirals with a mixture of white, pink, and pink and white striped straight piping. Start with the piping fold in the center, adding pleats as you spiral the piping out, covering raw edges as you go.

Block 6

12 This block has inward pleated spirals, with straight pink and white striped piping cut along the stripes instead of across them. Lay the piping with the fold along the edge of the octagon, and at the end of each side put in a tuck, so that the strip changes direction.

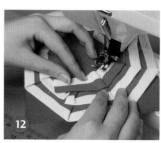

The bias piping gives the most amazing three-dimensional effects, and using striped fabric adds even more interest.

13 At the end of each piece of piping, fold the raw edges inside.

14 Stitch straight onto the next piece of piping, having folded its raw edges in too. The picture here shows the same technique but with the piping cut across the stripes.

Block 7

15 This block has an outward log cabin spiral, in either bias or straight piping, using alternate pink and white. Although you can start around a small imaginary square on the block base, the technique is shown with an interlocking center. Using four lengths of 2in (5cm) wide piping, center the first piece along the center crease, and stitch in place. Stitch the second piece perpendicular to the first one, as shown.

16 Stitch the third piece on as in step 15.

17 Stitch the fourth piece on as in step 15, but tuck one end under the first strip so that all the strips are interlocking in the same direction.

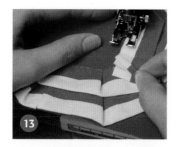

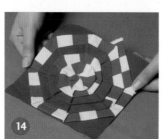

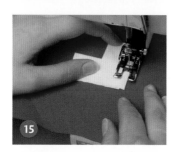

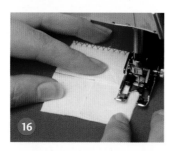

18 Lay a contrasting color of piping along one side and stitch and trim to the required length—leave the thread fixed but lift the presser foot off while you do this.

19 Lay the next piece across the corner of the square, parallel to the octagon edges.

20 Continue around, parallel to the octagon outline, until it has been filled in completely.

Block 8

21 This block is random log cabin, using bias or straight piping in pink and pink and white stripes. The piping is laid on at any angle as long as all the raw edges of the previous rounds are covered.

Block 9

22 This block is a Pineapple Log Cabin, using bias or straight piping in alternate pink and white. It is made as Block 7 but you make all the square edges on one round and then fill in the corners on that round in a different color.

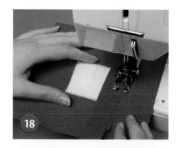

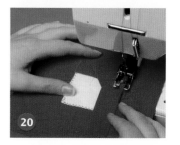

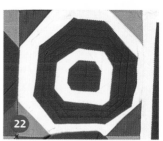

MAKING TRIANGLE CORNERS

23 Crease the 2½in (6.5cm) green squares diagonally. Lay a square on each corner, right sides together, and stitch along the diagonal, as shown. Or lay the folded square on the corner and pin in place so it will be caught into the seams as you join the blocks. If you do this you may need an extra strip of piping on each corner, so the green triangles cover all raw edges. Lift up any piping that may get caught under the triangles before they are stitched.

CONSTRUCTING THE QUILT

Following the block layout on page 106, join Blocks 1–9 in pairs, then join the pairs into blocks. Press the seams of pairs in opposite directions for easier joining. Lay these blocks on point between Blocks A–F. Pin the units into rows and stitch with ¼in (6mm) seams. For the border, join the smallest green triangles in pairs—one medium green and one light green—and add to the corner rows. Add the large green triangles along the edges of the other rows, the light green on the sides and the dark green on bottom and top. Press the seams in the opposite direction from row to row, then join the rows together. Stay stitch the edge of the quilt top with a

TIP
- *When making the triangle corners, place the light green squares on two opposite corners and the dark green on the corners in between. This makes a much more balanced design.*
- *I leave the ends of quilting threads loose on the border and then pull them up to correct the tension, with the quilt flat on the floor, before fastening them off.*

medium straight stitch, to stop the bias edges from stretching.

QUILTING

Hand stitch the outside of the large blocks and tie the small blocks in the center of each block of four. Quilt 6in (15cm) squares on the outer green triangles.

FINISHING

1 Trim off excess batting and trim the backing fabric so it is 1in (2.5cm) larger than the quilt all round. Cut the batting to the edge of the top, turn the backing fabric to the front and fold the raw edge under. Hand quilt through all layers.

2 Miter the corners by folding the corner diagonally and trimming off the point.

3 Fold the binding so the diagonal fold lies at 45° to the corner.

4 Fold the other edge in— it should butt to the first half of the diagonal fold —and continue quilting.

5 Hem the raw edges of the hanging tube strip. Position it right side out at the top of the back of the quilt and stitch in place along both the top and bottom edges.

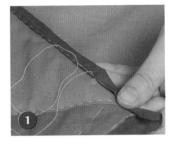

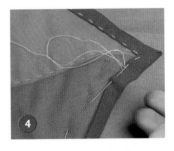

flip, flap, flop

I discovered the basics of this technique in 1982 when I was doing a project on snakes for my art foundation course. I began cutting triangles into my sketchbook pages, then developed a more formal method of measuring and folding several layers into one design. Years later I discovered Mola patchwork, and more recently Dutch artists have developed a technique of cutting and overlapping paper called Lacé. Eventually I tackled the technique in fabric. I first experimented using fabric stiffener but the fabric wrinkled up and didn't behave the way I wanted it to, so I fell back on fusible webbing. When I make my paper-cuts I make many holes on one piece of paper, but to simplify this project I have worked four holes on a small square, which can then be joined in a variety of ways.

Depending on the way you cut and arrange shapes, you cut flaps, flip them over or let them flop down. I have fused and stitched all these flaps down but I'm looking forward to attempting more floppy versions! I hope you have fun experimenting with other layouts, shapes and colorways.

Project by Louise Mabbs *Size: 23 x 40in (57.5 x 100cm)*

MATERIALS

- ❖ 1⅞yds (169cm) of 42in (105cm) wide black cotton fabric, cut as follows:
  18 pieces, each 6in (15cm) square
  2 pieces 23 x 40½in (57.5 x 101.5cm) for the background
- ❖ ½yd (45cm) of 42in (105cm) wide dark gray cotton fabric, cut into 13 pieces, each 6in (15cm) square
- ❖ ½yd (45cm) of 42in (105cm) wide medium gray cotton fabric, cut into 15 pieces, each 6in (15cm) square
- ❖ ⅜yd (34cm) of 42in (105cm) wide light gray cotton fabric, cut into 8 pieces, each 6in (15cm) square

- ❖ ⅝yd (58cm) of 42in (105cm) wide white cotton fabric, cut into 15 pieces, each 6in (15cm) square
- ❖ ½yd (45cm) of 42in (105cm) wide cotton fabric with a narrow black and white stripe, cut into 12 pieces, each 6in (15cm) square
- ❖ ¼yd (23cm) of 42in (105cm) cotton fabric with a narrow gray and white stripe, cut into 3 pieces, each 6in (15cm) square
- ❖ 60in (150cm) of 12in (30cm) wide fusible web, cut into 29 pieces, each 6in (15cm) square, for bonding squares together, plus small scraps to hold the layers together

COLOR LAYOUT

The color layout in my finished piece is a little more diverse than the simplified scheme for this project. Some of the blocks are five layers, others are six or seven layers deep. Double-sided squares are denoted by a slash sign between two colors.

BLOCK 1 – MAKE 4
Top layer: white/light gray
Second layer: medium gray/dark gray
Backing: black

BLOCK 2 – MAKE 2
Top layer: black/dark gray
Second layer: medium gray/light gray
Backing: white

BLOCK 3 – MAKE 2
Top layer: black/black and white stripe horizontal (when flipped it becomes vertical)
Second layer: dark gray/medium gray
Backing: black and white stripe vertical

BLOCK 4- MAKE 2
Top layer: white
Second layer: light gray
Third layer: medium gray
Fourth layer: dark gray
Backing: black

BLOCK 5- MAKE 2
Top layer: black/black and white stripe horizontal
Second layer: medium gray/dark gray
Third layer: black and white horizontal stripe/white
Backing: black

BLOCK 6 – MAKE 2
Top layer: white
Second layer: black and white stripe vertical/white
Third layer: medium gray/gray and white stripe horizontal (becomes vertical)
Backing: black

BLOCK 7 – MAKE 1
(DIAGONAL CROSS)
Top layer: black and white stripe vertical/black
Second layer: dark gray/medium gray
Third layer: black/black and white stripe horizontal
Fourth layer: gray and white stripe vertical
Backing: white

instructions ▸

1. The steps shown are for Block 1, but each block is constructed with the same techniques. Layer one white and one light gray square, wrong sides together, with a square of fusible webbing in between. Fuse the layers together. Repeat with the medium gray and dark gray square. Lay your fabrics in order: top layer—white/light gray; second layer—medium gray/dark gray; backing—black.

2. Press the top layer (white/light gray square) in half crosswise side to side

in each direction. Place your rotary ruler with the ¼in (6mm) line along the fold and cut parallel slits starting ¼in (6mm) from the center fold and ending ½in (15mm) from the outside edge.

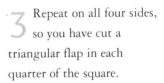

3. Repeat on all four sides, so you have cut a triangular flap in each quarter of the square.

4. Cut small triangles of fusible webbing and press one onto each corner of the cut flaps on the white side of the square.

5. Peel off the paper and press the triangular flap back, so that the light gray on the other side of the square is revealed.

6. The top layer of Block 1 is now complete; the picture shows the right side.

7. Turn the top layer over to the wrong side and press long thin strips of fusible webbing along the cross in the center, then peel off the backing paper.

8. Turn the top layer back over, so the right side is face up, and position over the second layer (medium gray/dark gray square) with the medium gray side uppermost. Press the top layer onto the second layer.

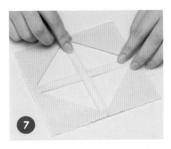

9 Place the ½in (15mm) measure on the ruler on the center fold lines. Using a rotary cutter, cut slits ¼in (6mm) away and parallel to the previous cut, going as near to the folded edge as you can, but being careful not to cut through it. Repeat on all four sides.

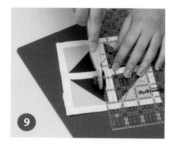

10 Continue the slit with sharp scissors, cutting just under the previous folded edge.

11 Press triangles of fusible webbing onto the top of the new flaps, and then press them down on top of the first folded triangles.

12 The second layer is complete; the photo shows it from the right side.

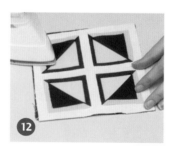

13 At this stage the flaps will pull the layers up at the outside corners, so press a very small square of fusible webbing on all the outside corners and carefully iron the layers together.

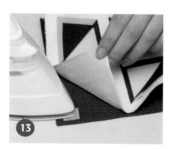

14 Turn the block over so the wrong side is face up and iron small squares of fusible webbing in the center and at all the outside corners, then peel off the backing paper.

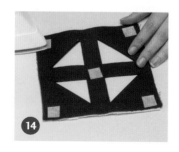

15 Lay the black square right side down on top of the wrong side of the block and iron across the fusible webbing areas to fix it in position.

16 Block 1 is now complete.

All the other blocks are assembled using the same methods, but following the order of color layering as detailed on page 116.

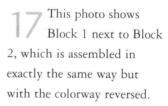

17 This photo shows Block 1 next to Block 2, which is assembled in exactly the same way but with the colorway reversed.

18 Block 7 starts with a diagonal cross, and each layer is stitched down with matching threads and a variety of zigzag stitch widths.

CONSTRUCTION

Trim each block square. On the right side of one piece of the black background fabric, lay the blocks out, right sides up, as in the block layout diagram, with a 1in (2.5cm) gap between each block and a 1½in (4cm) border around the sides and bottom. The top border should be about 3½in (9cm).

The central block is set on point and the fabric edges are decorated with zigzag stitching.

QUILTING

Appliqué the blocks to the background fabric. Machine stitch along the initial center fold lines with a short straight stitch. Stitch around the edge of each block with a wide zigzag, matching thread to the color of the block. Pull the thread ends through to the back and fasten them off.

FINISHING

With the wrong side of the appliquéd area facing up, press ½in (1.5cm) wide strips of fusible webbing onto the back of the panel, about ⅜in (9mm) in from all the raw edges and about 1in (2.5cm) above the top row of blocks. With right sides together, stitch the second piece of black background fabric to the appliquéd panel along the top short edge only. Press the seam open, then fold the backing fabric to the back of the appliqué panel along the seam line. Line up the raw edges on sides and bottom, peel off the backing paper of the fusible webbing and iron the layers together. Mark a line 2in (5cm) from the top seam and stitch across the line to make a hanging channel. Continue stitching all around the panel ¼in (6mm) in from the raw edge. Knot the stitching ends together and bury the ends between the layers.

jacob's ladder

The seeds of my interest in folding were set when I was ten and my Godfather gave me a book by Robert Harbin. Recently I found some tiny Jacob's Ladders folded in bright colors and wondered how you could make one in fabric. It needed a stiff fabric, colored on both sides, so I bonded two pieces of fabric together back to back. I used fast2fuse, which is a double-sided glued stiffening, but you can use a stiff craft interfacing with fusible webbing on both sides. Each unit is triangular in cross section, so the top section is flat at the front but has a series of triangular edges on the back.

Project by Louise Mabbs   Size: 22 x 35 x 2½ins deep (55 x 87.5 x 6.5cm)

MATERIALS

❖ ⅜yd (34cm) of 42in (105cm) wide cotton fabric in each colour, cut into six 2 x 28in (5 x 70.5cm) strips:

dark purple (1)

royal blue (2)

dark turquoise (3)

light turquoise (4)

medium green (5)

light green (6)

yellow (7).

orange/yellow (8)

orange (9)

red (10)

❖ ¼yd (22.5cm) of 42in (105cm) wide cotton fabric, in each colour, cut into four 2 x 28in (5 x 70.5cm) strips:

red purple (11)

maroon (12)

red/maroon (13)

❖ 2yds (180cm) of 28in (70.5cm) wide fast2fuse, or craft interfacing with fusible web on both sides

❖ Several spools of royal blue thread

❖ 8 small transparent rings for hanging

COLOR LAYOUT

Arrange the colors in sequence. An odd number means the colors come up against each other in different combinations. Pin the finished strips in the right order to avoid confusion.

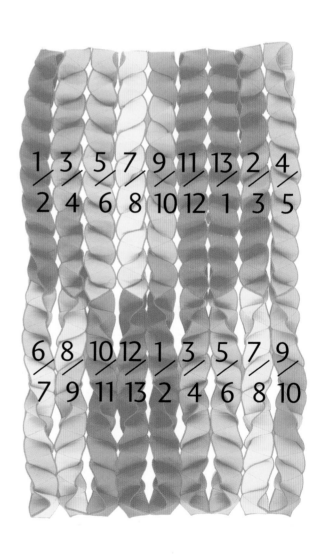

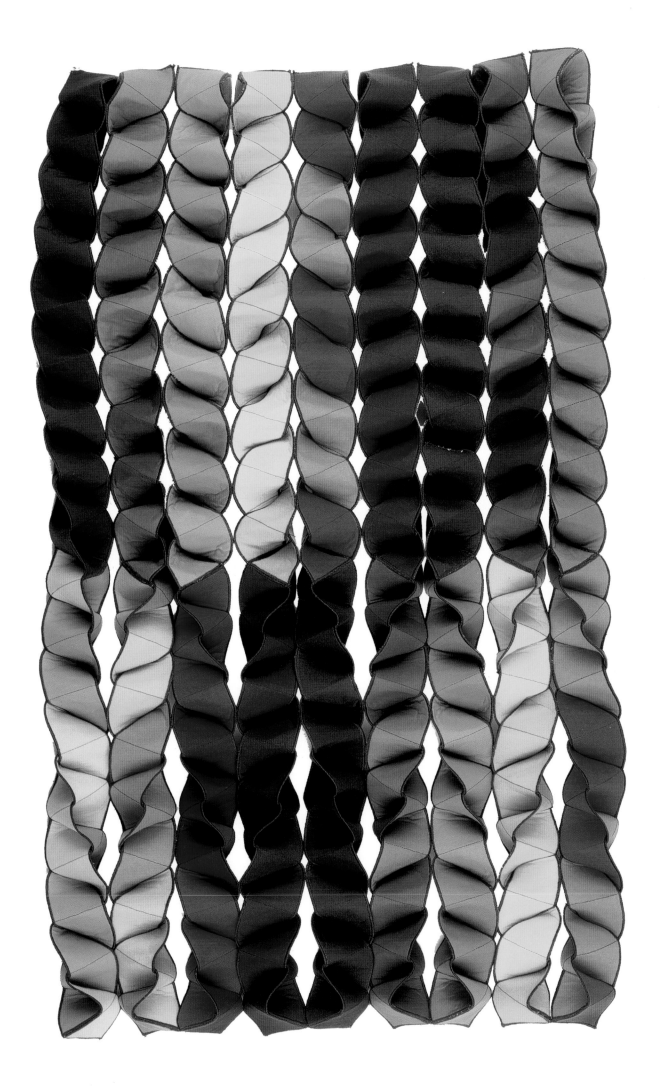

instructions ▶

1 Lay a long ruler with ends parallel to the sides of the fast2fuse and cut a 6in (15cm) wide strip. Cut a 4in (10cm) strip off this, then cut this into two 2in (5cm) wide strips—it is easier to handle working this way. You need 36 of these 2in (5cm) strips.

2 Press the first color onto one side of the fast2fuse or interfacing strip. Use Teflon or baking parchment to protect your iron so it doesn't get dirty.

3 Press the second color fabric to the other side of the fast2fuse strip. You need to make two sets of strips in each colorway.

4 Lay the bonded strips on a cutting mat and draw lines at 2in (5cm) intervals on one side only.

5 Machine stitch down each line in royal blue thread, using quite a short stitch length.

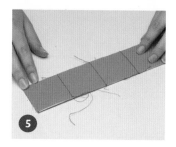

6 At the end of the line draw the thread along the edge of the strip and stitch across in the opposite direction. These threads will be hidden in subsequent stitching. If you prefer to chain piece the strips, sew each set of ends together and then the center lines, leaving a gap between the strips so

the threads can lock in between, and to prevent the edge stitches unravelling when you separate the strips.

7 Set your machine stitch to a narrow, open zigzag and stitch all around the strip, as shown on the top edge in the picture. Trim off the loose threads and ends. Set your machine to a wider satin stitch with a close-set length, and stitch all around the strip as shown here on the lower edge. Trim any loose ends.

8 Take the first two strips and place them one on top of the other at right angles. Pin the top ends with a safety pin to keep them together as you work. Start folding on the sewn lines to create a Jacob's Ladder.

9 Fold each strip away from yourself, each one under the other, alternating on each side. The first set needs to be folded clockwise, the second set needs to be folded counterclockwise. Repeat, alternating the direction of the folding.

10 Pin the far end of the strip with a safety pin. You may need to jiggle the strips a bit so you can fold them along the stitched fold lines, but don't worry, the structure will become

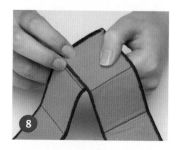

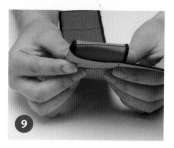

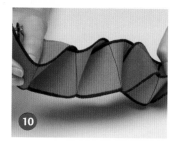

TIP
- *The top of the hanging is joined at every compartment. The bottom half is joined every fourth or fifth compartment so more twist is allowed.*

more solid when it is stitched together. Be careful to get the colors in the correct sequence.

11 Overcast the folded pairs together at each fold line—this will stabilize the structure.

12 Overcast the strip ends together along one edge. If you are adding several lengths, stitch the satin stitched ends together as required.

13 Safety pin the folded strips together in the correct color sequence. Sew the units together in the center of the front edge of each compartment using an overcast stitch—you may need to untwist the structure a little to get it to lie correctly.

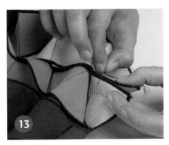

14 Join up all the units on one row. Join the corners of every two strips—this step shows the stitched ends from Step 13 being joined at the corners.

15 Sew hanging rings to the top of the units, by sewing two adjacent corners onto each ring. Hang on invisible fishing line so the wall hanging is suspended in midair.

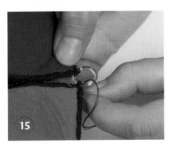

Detail of the twisted units in the lower half of the wall hanging. The top half is stitched together at every compartment, which gives a rather flatter surface with less twist.

CONSTRUCTING A QUILT

When putting your quilt together, you need to consider the arrangement of the blocks before you begin to sew. First look at the color, shape and scale of the blocks. With color, sort into dark, medium and light and try to balance the position of these across the whole quilt. Try to link colors progressively across the quilt—red/blue next to blue/green next to green/yellow—by taking one color to the adjacent block.

If all the blocks are similar colors, you can balance similar shapes instead. Those with designs based on an arc often look better in the top corners, and odd shapes can be positioned in the center column. Pictorial blocks are often best as the focal point in the center. Remember to balance both top and bottom, and side to side. It can often be helpful to look at the arrangement through half-closed eyes, or through a camera viewfinder to get a good impression of the overall effect.

Finally, if your quilt is to be used on a bed, consider which blocks will be across the top and which will hang down the sides, as this may affect the orientation of the block so that it is seen the correct way up.

JOINING BLOCKS WITHOUT SASHING

1 Pin two blocks together, placing the pins at right angles to the sewing line.

2 Sew together by machine or hand.

3 You can work in columns down the quilt and then sew the columns together.

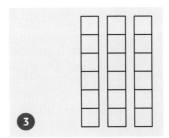

4 Alternatively you can work in rows across the quilt and then sew the rows together.

SASHING

Blocks are often put together with sashing between them. Where there are several types of block in one quilt—such as a sampler quilt—or where the blocks are very disjointed in design, sashing can bring a sense of unity. It can also be used to separate blocks with clashing colors. There are many ways of using sashing and the layout should complement the blocks themselves. A few of the most common are illustrated.

1. Sashed squares or plain trellis.
2. Sashed diamond or diamond trellis.
3. Square trellis with cornerstones.
4. Framed blocks with square trellis.

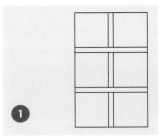

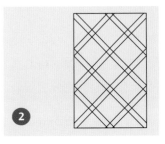

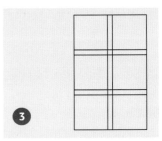

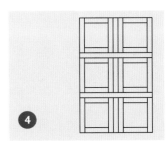

JOINING BLOCKS WITH SASHING

1 Plan the sashing layout before you begin. Add ½in (15mm) seam allowance to the sashing width—this will be the width of strip to cut for both A and B sashing.

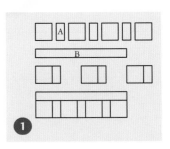

2 To find the length of an A strip, measure the side edge of a block with its seam allowance of ½in (15mm).

3 To find the length of a B strip, measure the top of a block, times this by the number of blocks in the row, then add the width of the A strip times the number of A strips. Finally add a seam allowance of ½in (15mm).

4 Cut the number of A and B sashing strips needed.

5 Sew the A strips to the top of the blocks, then join the blocks together into a row.

6 Join the rows of blocks with B strips in between.

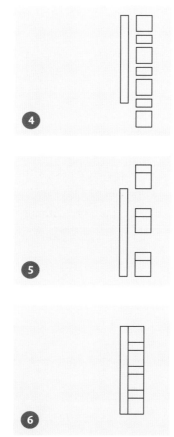

BORDERS

1 The easiest border around the outside is a simple square frame. Usually the shortest sides run across the longer, as shown in the top of this diagram, but sometimes quilts are constructed with the longest sides running across the shorter, as shown at the bottom of the diagram.

2 A mitered frame can be slightly more difficult, but using one of the simple methods shown on page 126 it is much easier.

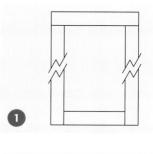

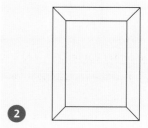

The square trellis sashing used in Fold-de-Roll, a sampler quilt by Hilary Burton using many of the techniques from this book, brings unity to the design.

SQUARE BORDERS

1 Measure the sides of the quilt and add ½in (15mm) seam allowance. On the two short sides, add the width of the borders, plus ½in (15mm) for the seam.

3 Cut the border strips. If you need to join pieces, make the join in the centre.

4 With right sides together, pin the centre of the side border to the centre of the quilt side. Pin outwards to the ends, making sure there are no puckers.

5 Sew the side borders on, stitching up to the end of the seam.

6 Fold the side borders out and press flat, with the seam towards the border. Sew top and bottom borders on, and press as for side borders.

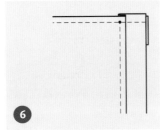

MITERED BORDERS

1 Measure all sides of the quilt and to each measurement add 3 times the border width—if the border is 3in (7.5cm) wide, add 9in (22.5cm).

2 Add the borders to the quilt as for Square Border, steps 3 and 4. Stitch the side borders, stopping at the seam allowance.

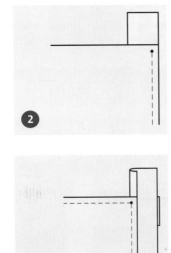

3 Sew the top and bottom borders, again stopping at the seam allowance.

MITER METHOD 1

1 Fold the quilt wrong sides together at the corner, at an angle of 45°. The border will hang down, with the wrong side facing.

2 Draw a line at 45° to the bottom edge of the border, through the marked point, as shown in the diagram. Stitch the borders together along this line, being careful not to catch the main quilt in your stitching.

3 Repeat on all four corners, then press the border back into position with the miter seams open and the block seams towards the border.

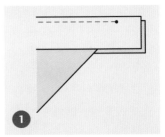

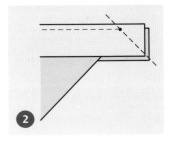

MITER METHOD 2

1 With wrong side facing, fold the top border tail back at 45° and crease a line as indicated, from the inner seam to the outer edge.

2 Fold the quilt at 45° across the corner and pin across the diagonal crease line in the border.

3 Stitch from the inner seam to the outer edge, then trim away the excess border fabric.

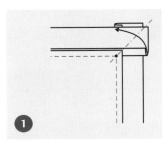

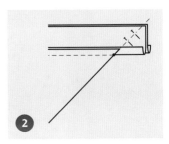

ADDING BACKING FABRIC

The backing fabric should be at least 1in (2.5cm) bigger all round on small quilts and 2in (5cm) on large ones. It needs to be stretched before the quilt is layered. Some people tack quilts in a radiating pattern, but this can distort the bias of the quilt so I use a technique adapted from upholstery.

Start by folding each edge of the quilt backing fabric in half and making a small crease. Lay fabric flat again and pin it into a carpet on the four folds with small headed pins, pulling the fabric taut without stretching it. Alternatively, you can use masking tape to fasten it to a table. Pin every 3–4in (7.5–10cm) on each side of these pins, alternating the vertical and horizontal sides so the stretch will be even in both directions. Take care not to stretch the corners.

Lay the wadding on top of the backing fabric—it will sit on the pins. Find the centers of the top edges, then lay the top on the wadding, matching the centers to the center folds in the backing fabric. Smooth the top out gently with your hands in both directions without stretching, pin with dressmaking pins and then tack or use small safety pins to hold the layers together.

Pin up and down and across the center lines, smoothing fullness out to the edge. On each quarter, pin 4–6in (10–15cm) parallel to the center lines in both directions, out to the edges. Tack a grid, following the pins in both directions. Remove the outer edge pins by feeling carefully for them in the wadding.

HANGING TUBES

In material matching the backing, cut a strip of fabric the width of your quilt and 9in (12.5cm) deep. Fold each end of the strip of fabric in by 1in (2.5cm) towards the wrong side, press and tuck the raw edge under the fold to make a double seam. Machine in place. Fold the strip in half lengthwise, wrong sides together, and pin and stitch along the length. Secure the ends of the seam with backstitching. The raw edges will fall between the tube and the quilt back and will not get ragged when poles go in and out. Press the tube flat with the seams open and lying on the reverse, halfway across the width. Lay the tube on the back of the quilt at the top, ⅝–1in (1.5–2.5cm) away from the binding, and pin the top edge into position. As you pin the lower edge, move it up by ⅝in (1.5cm) so there is extra fabric on the front side of the tube—when the pole is in place, the excess curves around the pole and prevents a distorted, curved effect on the front of the quilt. Stitch the tube to the quilt by hand, either with a spaced backstitch very close to the edge or with a small

The borders of Jean Martin's quilt, A Splash of Purple, are mitered, and both sashing and borders are hand tied rather than quilted.

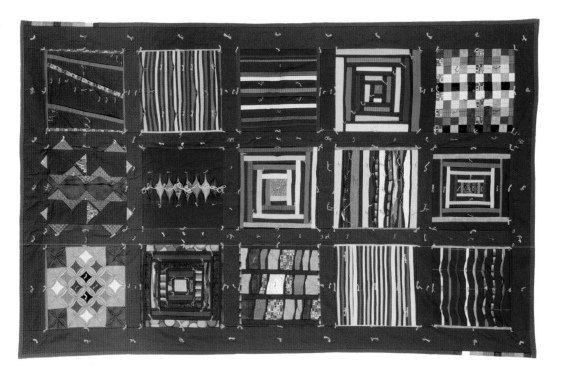

Bibliography

Clark, Mary Clare *Japanese Folded Patchwork* (Search Press, Tunbridge Wells, 2002)

Bryer Fallert, Caryl *A Spectrum of Quilts 1983–1995* (American Quilter's Society, Paducah, 1996)

Rayment, Jennie *Creative Tucks and Textures for Quilts and Embroidery* (Batsford, London, 2004)

Wright, Margaret K *Mitred Patchwork* (Batsford, London, 1986)

Edwards, Lynne *Through the Window and Beyond* (Martingale, Woodinville, 1995)

Yamaguchi, Makoto *Kusudama Ball Origami* (Japan Publications, Japan, 1990)

Fuse, Tomoko *Kusudama Origami* (Japan Publications, Japan, 2002)

Useful Organizations

British Origami Society, www.britishorigami.org.uk
2a The Chestnuts, Countesthorpe, Leicester, LE8 5LT

Origami USA, www.origami-usa.org
15 West 77th Street, New York, NY10024-5192

The Quilters' Guild of the British Isles, www.quiltersguild.org.uk
Room 190, Dean Clough, Halifax, HX3 5AX

The American Quilters' Society, www.americanquilter.com
PO Box 3290, Paducah, KY 42002-3290

The Authors

Louise Mabbs has been sewing since she was eight years old. She studied textiles at Winchester in England, and soon developed a particular interest in quilting. She now makes commissioned pieces, teaches, and writes on quilting and patchwork for magazines. This is her first book, but her work has been featured in several books by other authors.

Wendy Lowes trained as a graphic artist and worked in a London advertising agency, specializing in three-dimensional work. She developed an interest in textile art in the 1960's and studied embroidery at Windsor in 1987. After two years of research into fabric folding techniques, she gained a Diploma in Stitched Textiles followed by a BA Hons. Degree in Art and Design. She has been teaching and lecturing on Origami Techniques in Fabric since 1997.

Acknowledgments

With thanks to: Marie Clayton, for commissioning us to do this book; Michael Wicks, for the beautiful photography; Carly and Abby, the hand models; and Louise Leffler for her wonderful page design.

In addition I would like to thank

- Don and Wendy Bruff, my Godfather and his wife, who gave me my first origami book for my 10th birthday—little did they know it would lead to this.
- Mum and Dad for encouraging me to follow my heart in my career choices and who, along with my in-laws, Mike and Angela Mabbs, held the fort while I finished the work.
- Ken, Jessica and family, for permission to dedicate the book to Ruth, who was a jeweler, belly dancer, singer, waved her colorful banners in worship and brought great spiritual wisdom to all who knew her.
- Alex, Zachary, Joshua, and Isabella for letting me off the housework so I could be in my studio. I have a lot to make up!
- Val Palin (neé Moberley), my school needlework teacher, the first to really push and encourage me, who died far too early from breast cancer.
- Vera Grey, my needlework-teacher aunt who encouraged me all the way.
- All my quilting/origami/embroidery friends, and especially my students Jean Martin, Hilary Burton, Joanna Hird, Gloria Phillipps, Diane Miller Ingham and Marie Garret, who sounded out and tested some of the ideas.
- God, for giving me my gifts and ambitions.
- Wendy, my co-writer.

LM

I would like to acknowledge the late Margaret Darby, who introduced me to Cathedral Window folded patchwork.

Also, thanks to Jan Beaney and Jean Littlejohn, who encouraged me all through the City& Guilds and Diploma in Stitched Textiles courses.

WL